BOSS LESSONS

LEADERSHIP SKILLS AND
MINDFULNESS HABITS TO
TRANSFORM YOUR LIFE AND
SAVE YOUR CAREER

*Mannon,
I hope you find
this amusing and
helpful!*

PARKSIDE bks

PARKSIDE BOOKS
HOLT, MICHIGAN

Mickey Hadick

Boss Lessons: Leadership Skills And Mindfulness Habits To Transform Your Life And Save Your Career

Copyright © 2015 Mickey Hadick

All rights reserved. No part of this book may be used or reproduced in any manner whatsoever without written permission.

First Printing, *January, 2016*

Amazon Kindle Edition ASIN: B019LUI4M0
ISBN-13: 978-1522979685
ISBN-10: 1522979689
BISAC: Business & Economics / Leadership

Cover design by Michael Reibsome

Interior design by Mickey Hadick

Published by Parkside Books

www.parksidebooks.net

BOSS LESSONS

MICKEY HADICK

Table of Contents

1 Why You Should Read This Book...1
2 How to Make the Most of This Book...8
3 Mindfulness Habits for Fun and Profit...17
4 Lead Yourself to Greater Success...23
5 Learn Everything You Need to Know the Easy Way............................31
6 Laundry List of Leadership Styles..39
7 Nice-to-Haves in a Leader's Personality..51
8 Ought-to-Haves in a Leader's Character...56
9 Joe Schmoe and Aunt Flo Become CEO...61
10 What's Different That Doesn't Come Down to Bosses Being Bossy?..67
11 Inspire Followers Rather than Manipulate the Meek...........................75
12 How to Lead a Specific Person..83
13 What If I'm Surrounded by Butthead Bosses?.....................................87
14 The Most Important Thing a Leader Can Do..93
15 Improve Leadership at Your Organization in a Meaningful Way........99
16 Become the Leader You Were Meant to Be.......................................103
17 Next Steps...107
18 A Parting Gift in Thanks..109
19 About the Author..110
20 Acknowledgments..111
21 References..113

1

WHY YOU SHOULD READ THIS BOOK

"The task of leadership is not to put greatness into humanity, but to elicit it, for the greatness is already there."

—John Buchan

Why Bother?

Do you wonder if you should even care about leadership skills? Do you feel like one of those extras in a low-budget office comedy, at the mercy of a butthead boss who knows nothing about leadership and yet controls your career?

Even if you do care about leadership, are you convinced that some people are born leaders? Or that the way things are is the way things are meant to be? And that it's probably for the best that you just do what you've been told, no matter how stupidly your boss may be laying waste to the company.

Boss Lessons—Leadership Skills and Mindfulness Habits to Transform Your Life and Save Your Career will help you understand that leaders are made, not born. You can develop the skills of great leaders just like you can develop skills to play a sport, a musical instrument, or to use a computer.

Can't do any of those things either? Well can you walk? Because if you have the use of your legs, and you know how to walk, then you are capable of learning. And if you can learn to walk, you can learn to lead. Once you understand that, then you can hone and optimize your leadership skills.

Most people that walk have no idea how they learned to do it. But we definitely face-planted a couple of times, and sat down hard several times. But we got up and tried again. We were motivated at a very basic level to move independently.

Now you're older, and you may think that some people were born with exactly everything they needed to be a leader. Even if they suck at leadership, but they just happen to be in charge and act all bossy, you may assume that since birth it was inevitable that they would someday be a leader.

Not true.

Those leaders, bossy bosses and butthead bosses alike, may not be aware of what they went through to develop their leadership skills any more than you or I are aware of what we went through to develop our ability to walk. Those ignorant bastards are completely oblivious of how they learned such an important skill.

But this book will tell you how to develop those skills.

Boss Lessons will:
- Identify your natural leadership style
- Help you assess the skills you have
- Teach other leadership styles
- Inspire you to develop the habits necessary to live a mindful, intentional life

If you apply the lessons in this book, I guarantee that your leadership skills and intentional living habits will improve. And once that happens, you will begin to dictate the terms of your life and grasp the dreams that today seem out of reach.

But What About Butthead Bosses?

There are some innate personality attributes that lend themselves to leadership. Specifically, if someone is confrontational or argumentative, they may be perceived as having leadership potential. We encounter a great number of bosses who are more a-hole than A-team. This is because confrontation is occasionally needed in leadership roles. But people who don't understand the other demands of leadership focus on confrontation and embrace it. "They seem bossy, so let's make them the boss."

It seems that every company has enough dysfunctional stupidity in their culture to give rise to a butthead boss. Part sadist, part moron, they berate subordinates, insist on overtime, and then ask for help sending an email with an attachment. People scurry from their teams, and somehow the moron survives layoffs, only to emerge after a reorganization in another, more vulnerable part of the company.

Many years ago I worked for a computer systems integrator, a company that built mainframes and sold them to big business or government agencies. Millions of dollars changed hands regularly. I was at a branch office of that company, and the Branch Manager was a large man of few words. He reminded me of the giant from Jack and the Beanstalk, and he roamed the halls with a fee-fie-fo-fum vibe, looking to and fro as he passed through our cubicles on one of his regular inspections.

He was made the Branch Manager because he sold the first mainframe for this company into the state government. That had been years before I arrived. Since that first sale, he had ruled that little empire in the clouds while the contract with the state laid golden eggs.

Everyone in the office deferred to his judgment on all matters, unwilling to challenge the giant. I had no desire to be Jack to his Giant. I was there as a computer guy helping the salesman close deals.

The salesmen all dreaded their meetings with him. He wanted to know what sales they had closed recently, and what sales they planned on making in the near future. All other matters were secondary. Salesmen (and women) who did not sell were relegated to less fertile lands. (I doubt that the sales people dreaded it as much as I believed they might—they were all cut from the same cloth, and once they realized their customers weren't buying or that the boss didn't like them, they often left for higher commission positions—but I found it to be oppressive.)

If the salesmen were bothered at all, I was in mortal fear. I once made the mistake of visiting the men's room at the same time as the Branch Manager (and not simply because of the lack of ventilation). As we dried our hands, he invited me to his office.

"Mickey," he said, "what do you do around here?"

I explained how I used my education on computers and programming to assist the salesman.

"But what do you do to earn your keep?"

I mumbled something about assisting the salesmen.

He nodded and sent me away with a wave of his hand.

From then on, I took my bathroom breaks at the gas station down the road.

If you are conflict averse, and avoid confrontation whenever possible, do not put aside this book just yet. I, too, avoided confrontation. I steered clear of all conflict. Even as I played ice hockey—one of the most violent of sports—in my youth, I played meekly. I was afraid of hitting too hard lest a fight break out. Then, once I began to understand what leadership demands, and how intentional living offers so many rewards, I began to embrace confrontation, and found ways to resolve conflict that did not avoid the important issues. Unfortunately, I learned this long after I stopped playing hockey.

One of my greatest discoveries on my leadership journey has been a courage which enables me to take charge of my own life. This courage instilled a confidence in me and others that, while we might make some mistakes along the way, we will solve the problem at hand. If obstacles stand in our way, we will clear them, resolving conflicts without exacerbating.

I embarked on an effort to understand what made some people leaders—not necessarily so I could be in charge like them—but rather, so I could take action with the confidence, determination and grit that I saw in them.

I wanted to make myself a better person and lead a more enjoyable life. I was tired of waiting for promotions to make things better for me.

What I wanted to do, more than anything else, was to become a leader that could challenge butthead bosses and thrive.

What I have found, and what you will find as well, is that if you develop your leadership skills and master the habits of living a mindful, intentional life, you will:

- No longer wonder what will happen when you're faced with great challenges
- Positively impact the lives of your friends, family, and coworkers
- Achieve previously unreachable dreams in your life

How Long Will This Take?

Finally, Boss Lessons will show you how to develop those leadership skills with as few as 15 minutes of practice a day. Just like when you first learned to walk, you did not walk very well for quite a long time. A toddler is a toddler for a couple of years. Young ones don't toddle because they're wearing a diaper. They toddle because it takes that long to walk well.

You are undertaking a completely new approach to your problems,, and ultimately, you're finding your place in the world. You will strengthen new muscles as you learn, and forget about other muscles you don't need anymore.

Your adult brain does not learn the way an infant's brain learns, and you must consciously develop the proper habits for success. Except this time you probably don't have your mother or father holding your hand.

You must do this all by yourself, but Boss Lessons shows you how.

You must develop a new habit when you start your journey, and it's this habit that will be like those parental hands that lifted you up off of your butt when you fell down oh so many years ago.

BOSS LESSONS

The habit is mindfulness, and it works best when you spend just a few minutes a day planning what you will do, and then reviewing how it went later on.

It's as simple as putting one foot in front of the other. The key is doing it over and over again.

Simply putting one foot mindfully in front of the other opens up a world of possibilities for yourself. If nothing else, you could walk from here to Lake Titicaca.

When you get there, look me up. I'll buy you a cup of Bolivian coffee, and together we'll keep watch on the horizon for butthead bosses.

2

HOW TO MAKE THE MOST OF THIS BOOK

"True leaders understand that leadership is not about them but about those they serve. It is not about exalting themselves but about lifting others up."

—Sheri L. Dew

The Very First Thing is Keep a Journal

The first baby step I hope you take is to begin journaling. Journaling is useful in the adoption of many habits, and in gaining an understanding of your own mind. When trying to learn a new skill, journaling is especially powerful.

I was introduced to journaling by a friend who was going through a difficult time. She described journaling as a way to see her thoughts in a way that made sense where once there was confusion.

My research into the practice proved to me what it is about the act of journaling that helps: searching for and selecting particular words to express yourself. Some of you may be thinking, "well duh," but the point is that you can approach a journal as a simple log of events;

i.e., this happened, then that happened. Taking time to careful consider what happened and how that made you feel is what matters.

Writing down your thoughts forces them through a different part of the brain. When you read them back, it puts those thoughts through yet another part of the brain. The change in perspective is what cuts the confusion and offers clarity. You catch a glimpse of your thoughts in a particular moment. You see what you were going through, and can learn from it. You gain perspective.

I have since used journaling to gain much greater understanding of myself, my eating habits, my creative writing, and my various other projects.

Please note that the journals themselves do not need to persist like family heirlooms or be protected in the ark of the covenant. You may find that you have no interest in the journal once the changes are apparent, or the project is done.

It's entirely up to you because it's your journal, and you are the only intended audience. Or are you?

Intermediate Journaling

Journaling is a private affair, but you may also use it to deal with specific people as if engaged in conversation with them. For instance, your boss. You may have several things you want to express to your boss. Your chest may be heavy with the burden of holding back the comments you want so very badly to say to their face. These are the proverbial bones to pick. But that conversation may be too intense for either of you to deal with.

Address your boss in a journal entry as if writing them a letter (a strongly-worded letter) or speaking directly. Repeat this exercise until you have unburdened yourself of these troubles. Make it conversational, as if they were at the table with you, listening.

Your stress may be relieved as a result, allowing you to think more clearly about the best course of action.

This exploits the phenomenon of the physical body experiencing a fictional event as if it actually happened. Skeptical that writing in a journal can have this effect? Have you ever watched a horror movie and been frightened out of your seat? Have you read a book and been choked up, or laughed out loud? Those false experiences led to true physical effects on your mind and body.

Journaling can be a truly therapeutic experience for dealing with difficult people in your life. You'll need to work on that habit so that you can get into the moment, just as the early part of a movie will suck you in. It's a setup for a pay off.

But in this case, you're setting yourself up to feel better.

What Sort of Journal is Good For Journaling?

Over the past few years I have experimented with spiral notebooks, string-bound theme books, leather bound journals, and cardboard bound Moleskine and Moleskine clones. In short, whatever brings you joy in that moment is fine for your journal. This journal is for you. Anyone that judges your character based on your choice of writing material is an ass and not worth the hassle of explaining your journal choice to.

If you're being cautious and practical, use a cheap spiral notebook.

If you can afford a leather bound journal with heavy paper, indulge yourself. You're worth it. You're even worth a decent pen.

But the Moleskine and Moleskine clones work great. They have very nice paper, and can last for years if you need them to.

Side Mention About the SELF Journal

At the time of this writing, I have ordered (but not yet received) a SELF journal. The SELF journal has formatted pages to encourage your ability to focus on a single purpose. Something like that might be ideal for developing leadership skills. (I'll let you know once I've tried it.)

It also has quotes, aphorisms and advice to support the adoption of an intentional life. I'm currently using a printed-out version of the journal to write this book. That's also proof that a stack of paper works just fine for a journal, and maybe none of us actually needs something as nice as the SELF journal.

That said, I ordered two of them anyway. If you're interested, visit their website at www.bestself.co†.

Set Aside Time Pretty Much Everyday, Forever

Learning any new skill as an adult requires dedicated time each day, and a chance for your brain to process it as you sleep. You're much better off setting aside 15 minutes everyday rather than working on something for two hours on Saturday and giving it a miss the rest of the week.

Our brains have a property called neuroplasticity that allows us to adapt to changes in our environment and learn new skills. Without it, we'd be limited to reacting to stimulation the way lizards and spiders watch television—they see the lights and hear the sounds, but they don't get the jokes.

Neuroplasticity changes the dominant pathways between neurons dynamically, using a substance called myelin to wrap neuron pathways, kind of like greasing the skids to make moving a heavy object easier. With practice and repetition, neuroplasticity enforces the learned skill making that skill second nature. It's how we learned to walk, and it's how we learn to run, and it's how we learn to drive a car.

This topic is worthy of the numerous books available, but for a solid introduction by a leading authority, read Dr. David Perlmutter's article, "Making Connections: The Gift of Neuroplasticity"†. You must challenge your brain repeatedly, practice effectively, and pay careful attention to the activity. It's not enough to just do something. You must also actively engage your mind or the brain calls bullshit and doesn't waste time building up the pathways with myelin.

This book is about learning techniques to care for yourself, increasing mindfulness, and developing leadership skills. These are much higher level concepts than walking or running, but the brain will work with you to learn them if you pay attention to what you're doing.

In *The Talent Code* by Daniel Coyle†, there is an excellent explanation of how important it is to pay attention while practicing, and to practice doing things correctly. For if you practice bad habits, the brain will learn the bad habits and make them second nature.

If you struggle dealing with your boss, or are frustrated because you never seem to figure out how to advance at your job, you may have stuck yourself with bad habits that have become second nature. You may not be aware of the subtleties involved, and that's why it's important to find a mindfulness activity: it raises your awareness of the present situation.

Wait, Why is it Important to Raise Awareness of the Present?

By raising your awareness of the present moment, you may notice the mistakes you're making (or about to make) that lead to troubles or frustration with your career.

By noticing the mistakes, you can begin to practice correcting them. That may involve catching yourself saying inappropriate or unhelpful things and retracting them. I have often said, "I'm sorry, that was dumb. I should have said..."

The beautiful part is that people often react positively to such humility. They recognize their own humanity in our mistake, and admire our ability to admit it.

Little do they know, it's for our selfish reasons.

Embrace Adult Learning

Malcolm Shepherd Knowles† (1913–1997) was an educator with a particular passion for the topic of adult learning. He popularized the term andragogy (like pedagogy, but for adults—and hey, I don't think the term andragogy is all that popular outside of academic circles) and documented some assumptions and principles about adult learning.

Pay attention to these and it may set the right mood for taking full advantage of your developing leadership skills.

Knowles's Assumptions about Adults Ready to Learn are:

- **Self-concept**: you realize you are a self-directed being, and not someone's kid anymore
- **Adult Experience**: you have a lifetime of experience to draw upon to enrich your ability to learn
- **Readiness**: your role in society (office worker, parent, or whatever) is relevant to why you want to learn something
- **Orientation**: if you're going to bother learning something, it's because you want to use it now to solve a problem
- **Motivation**: your motivation is internal

Adult Learning Applied

To recap the above points, if you recognize that you are in charge of your own life, and you have all of your life experiences to help you, and you have a very good reason to learn now, then you have a great chance of mastering whatever you set your mind to do.

But if you think you have to learn this because I'm telling you to, or because someone else thinks you should, or that it won't help you even if you do learn, then you will have a hard time mastering this approach.

If you're not sure, I urge you to take a couple of hours and think about what is in your best interests, and if reading any further in this book will serve those interests.

It's better to succeed when it's your focused attention that leads to the achievement. If you try something half-assed but somehow it works anyway, you may not be able to repeat it. You'll sap your own motivation thinking it was just luck, and there was no reason to bother in the first place.

Intentional living can take you anywhere you want to go. But you will have to pay attention.

More About Journaling, Neuroplasticity and Adult Learning

The first time I heard of this process was from my friend, Tom Matt, on his podcast called Boomers Rock, and then also in his book, *Maximize the Quality of Your Life*†, discussing Dr. George Bartzokis.

For more proof than that, read *The Talent Code* by Daniel Coyle†. (Yes, this is a repeat reference.)

It is mentioned in that book that many high-achievers use journals to track their progress. Peyton Manning (football), Andy Warhol (artist), and Oprah Winfrey (media) journaled.

In *The Progress Principle*†, authors Teresa Amabile and Steven Kramer suggest that journaling can improve focus, planning, and personal growth.

Finally, another important book about adult learning is *Mindset* by Carol Dweck†. It is one of the books that turned my fanciful daydreaming into specific projects of self-improvement and creative development.

I have kept various journals over the years. One for tracking my health, another for exercise, and others for creative writing, work, and personal projects. The entries are as diverse as stream-of-consciousness narrative, lists of ideas, or doodles and diagrams.

Summary

That's it—set aside time every day, keep a journal, and learn like an adult who is ready to make use of what you learn.

3

MINDFULNESS HABITS FOR FUN AND PROFIT

"You can discard most of the junk that clutters your mind—things that exist only there —and clear out space for yourself."

—Marcus Aurelius

Mindful of What?

Mindfulness means to experience the current moment with your full attention. It's remarkably difficult to do because of the way our brains work and the many distractions our world presents. But mindfulness is khe one thing that can make you more effective, more productive, and happier all at the same time.

Mindfulness means to pay attention to what you're doing. I have trouble some times keeping my focus even while typing a sentence. Once I've decided what the sentence should say, and I begin typing the words, my mind may wander to the next sentence, or some entirely different topic even as another part of my brain directs my fingers to tap away at the keyboard.

Even while driving a car, it is possible for the conscious mind to wander even as another part of the brain keeps the car moving. The brain has a remarkable ability to turn repetitive tasks into mindless scripts and play them as needed like computer programs. But if we turn every part of our life into a mindless script, we turn ourselves into more of a robot.

Even if we resist that urge to make everything a mindless script, our attention is distracted from all over our cultural landscape. There are billboards along the road, advertisement on the cars on the road, and advertisements on the radio inside the car on the road.

When we browse the Internet, we are navigating a minefield of pop-up advertisements. Each one calls out for our attention.

If you work in an office setting, you likely sit in a cubicle and are subject to distraction all day long. Every joke told in the office calls for your attention. Every gathering in the hall to solve a problem calls for your attention. Every time someone wonders aloud if it's time to check on the donut situation in the break room calls for your attention.

Our own thoughts and worries about the past, present, and future steal our attention away from what we are doing.

In a world that threatens our focus at every single moment of the day, how are we to stay focused on a single task? How will we ever get anything done when we're expected to pay attention to everything?

Anyone Can Be More Mindful

I know I'm a flawed person. Among my many flaws, the greatest is a compulsive need to be clever about many, many things. I have tried to master music, literature, writing, game development, computer programming, my job, and my family. I have tried so many things that I never got very good at any of them.

Some multitasking is inevitable, but I made it all so very much worse for myself by chasing so many things at once. This went on for nearly 20 years. I realize now that it was a major source of frustration. What is worse, I inflicted that frustration on myself.

I fell victim to our distraction-filled world, but I also didn't care about any one thing enough to focus on it long enough to master it.

What Mindfulness Can Do For You

The world we know is known through our perceptions. Our minds assemble all that we perceive into a model of reality that is ultimately our own. At the same time, our brains process what has happened in the past, such as mistakes we made, insults we suffered, and opportunities missed. We also try to identify dangers ahead while planning how to get our next donut and cup of coffee. There's a lot going on between our ears at any given moment.

Our minds are designed to handle several things at once. If that's the way we're built, what's so bad about letting it happen? Why not willingly chase several things at once? Maybe one of them will work out.

But I know my effectiveness is limited when trying to multitask. If you're struggling to keep up, what can you do to push ahead at anything?

How can we use our mind differently than how we use it already?

We must increase our capacity for mindfulness. In being mindful, we pay more attention to the present moment, and the task at hand. In being mindful, we can decide what is most important to accomplish at any given moment in order to achieve a particular goal.

Mindfulness allows focus, and focus allows accomplishment.

But what does it mean to be mindful?

To be mindful is to forgive ourselves for past mistakes in order to move ahead with our life.

To be mindful is to forgo worry about the future and trust that we will rise to challenges as they are presented.

To be mindful is to be present in the moment.

In reference to this chapter's epigraph, Marcus Aurelius, writing in what became his Meditations, says that clearing out the mind of unnecessary thoughts leaves room for yourself. He's describing a state of mindfulness.

To become mindful, we must teach ourselves to be that way. We know the world is designed to distract us. So look first within yourself.

This is How to Be More Mindful

There are a few ways to learn mindfulness.

Meditation is arguably the most direct. Specifically, the breath-awareness and body scan meditation can lead to increased capacity for mindfulness. In fact, it is often called "mindfulness meditation."

The short description of this meditation technique is to sit quietly in a comfortable position at a quiet time with limited distractions. Set a timer for at least five minutes. Then close your eyes and focus on your breathing. Pay attention to how your lungs fill up and how your breath pushes out. If any other thoughts come up, tell yourself that you don't have to worry about that other thing right now. You only have to think about your breathing.

Meditation may be a challenge for extroverts. But it is possible for certain repetitive activities to be used as a basis for mindfulness training. Tennis, for instance, can increase your ability to focus on the present if you refrain from chatting while exchanging volleys with a partner. If you focus on the ball, your stroke, and preparation for the return, you are training your mind to be present in the moment.

I have also been told that golf can be that way, but I've never seen anyone play more than a couple of holes without feeling frustrated or being distracted by other golfers. Also, the beer cart may stop by and tempt you.

Sailing a boat in calm conditions can be a basis for mindfulness training once you have mastered the sport. There are constant adjustments needed, and it demands the skipper's presence in the moment.

Walking can also be used as a form of meditation if you pay attention to the current environment and you focus on being present in the moment.

What got me started was a recommendation to read *Peace Is Every Step: The Path of Mindfulness in Everyday Life* by Thich Nhat Hanh†. In it, Hanh explains the benefits of living a mindful life, and teaches you how to integrate the training into every aspect of your life.

I Tried Meditating Once But...

I have talked to people about meditating and they were frustrated because they couldn't seem to quiet their mind long enough to pay attention even a single breath. Thoughts, memories, and forgotten chores flooded into their mind. They found it exhausting.

This is normal.

The flood of thoughts is very typical. The point of meditating, in my opinion, is not to achieve a higher level of consciousness that puts you into a state of nirvana—although this is a nice benefit if it happens. The point of meditating is to train your brain to focus on your experience in this moment. The fact that you suffer the flood of distracting thoughts is the reason why it's important to practice meditation.

You need to strengthen your brain's ability to focus so that you can increase your mindfulness.

I meditate every morning as part of my daily routine, but I also apply Hanh's teachings throughout my day. I implore you to at least experiment with meditation, or to integrate a mindful activity into your day. The benefits are small but immediate.

However, the accumulated effect over time is enormous and life changing. Increasing your capacity for mindfulness will make the remaining chapters in this book of much greater value.

The combination of mindfulness and leadership skills can be transformational.

4

LEAD YOURSELF TO GREATER SUCCESS

"Leadership should be born out of the understanding of the needs of those who would be affected by it."

—Marian Anderson

I Thought My Boss Was My Leader

A business is a place where efficient management is demanded, profit is pursued, and control is expected. Unfortunately, a business is not a place where leadership is prized or nurtured. Leadership is often claimed by those in charge, but the effectiveness of that leadership is omitted from a profit-and-loss report. And yet we all crave leadership. We arrive on the first day hoping that the managers know what they are doing, and where they need to go to achieve success. We look to the managers for guidance and inspiration.

Instead, managers tell us what procedures to follow, where to sit, and when we are expected to arrive in the morning. Guidance and inspiration may be promised, but is rarely delivered. We are mostly left to guide ourselves towards completing our tasks.

Where I Started

My first full-time job was with Burroughs (now Unisys). At the time (1986), it was a huge traditional corporation with a massive, central staff that controlled operations and meted out decision-making authority on an as-needed basis. I was one of over 60,000 employees.

This was what seemed to be the hey-day of American business, and used a matrix management style: numerous departments to deal with the various aspects of operations, and numerous levels of leadership to handle each step in the respective processes.

I assumed that if I showed how clever I was and worked hard, I would be promoted into the upper levels of management.

My first boss, Stanley Fenner, offered advice to me as a new hire. What he told me was to make myself invaluable to my immediate boss, and "if he gets promoted, you'll probably get promoted along with him." I don't think he was being disingenuous and trying to get me to do all of his work. I believe that it was his philosophy for advancement. He was suggesting that doing that one thing would serve me well for my entire career. And maybe that works great for some people.

I don't think it helps develop any concept of leadership, either for yourself or for the company. But it was the best suggestion I had when I left college.

Where I Went to College

I attended the University of Michigan in Ann Arbor. I thought getting a degree from there would make me a leader if only because it's in our fight song ("...Hail, hail, to Michigan the leaders, the best.")

Actually, the truth is that I didn't think about leadership. I thought I'd get a good job if I got that degree (it worked). My degree was Computer Engineering, and I spent the entire time at Michigan working very hard to get through those classes. I focused on my grade point average, and used that first job as my reward for the hard work.

At Michigan, I learned a great deal about how to build computers, create operating systems, and write software programs. But I didn't learn any particular leadership skills. There were certainly opportunities for that on campus, and had I realized the importance of leadership for directing my own destiny, maybe I would have taken advantage of those opportunities.

That mistake is definitely on me, but I was oblivious. And I don't think I'm alone in this. I had accepted the default plan of college first, job second, success eventually. No one had ever hit me over the head with the need to take care of my own destiny. Which brings me to where I came from.

Where I Came From

My parents both worked at one company for their entire working lives, 40 years for my father at Cleveland Electric Illuminating, and 30 years for my mother at Cleveland Trust. They sometimes talked about promotions and management, but it was not an emphasis in our house. Sports and family were of greater importance (and in a different book, those topics could each be argued to be a source of personal satisfaction).

As I approached college, my father was adamant that I should get an engineering degree so that I could find a job. His main concern was that I should find a job with benefits so that I could take care of myself and a family. (Again, fine sentiments.)

So I was very proud of getting into Michigan (and I still am). I thought that once I got that degree and got that job that I could coast my way up the corporate ladder and things would just work out.

Where I've Been

Since that first job, I've worked at similar companies for thirty years. For lack of a better philosophy, I've approached each job with the advice Stan gave me back in 1985—make myself invaluable to my immediate boss and hope she gets promoted.

That probably has worked great for some, but mostly I've been solving other people's problems.

A Funny Thing Happened on the Way to the Executive Suite

I began to believe that I wasn't cut out for leadership. I thought that maybe I wasn't worthy of knowing whatever was the elusive secret of leadership magic. I was beginning to self-loathe.

I'm a Fraud, and It's Just a Matter of Time Before the Boss Gets Rid of Me

A little bit of self-loathing goes a long way. Very few of us deserve self-loathing but, even if we do, we should offer ourselves some extra self-compassion. That's actually a fairly tall order if you don't even realize the source of your self-loathing. (I'll address that level of emotional intelligence some other time.)

I began to think that I wasn't worthy of being a leader. I wondered if I deserved to have a job at all. I questioned my career choices, my degree, and my very existence.

Once the mind begins that line of questioning, it's difficult to stop. I understand why some people turn to destructive distractions—gambling, alcohol, Adam Sandler movies.

The solution is as simple as learning how to walk. But the trick is to allow yourself that moment of innocence, like that of a newborn baby. You must accept the fact that you don't know how to walk, and to be excited about the learning you have to do.

Become the Leader You Would Follow to the Ends of the Earth, and There You Will Find Success

Learn how to lead, and then lead yourself.

I finally understood that I might be able to learn how to act leaderly when I observed a number of people being promoted into supervisory positions during a reorganization.

There were a dozens of people in what I'll call cubicle positions at the office. I was one of them. We were considered professional status, and for every dozen or so such workers there was a manager.

I noticed that, of the people chosen to be supervisors, none of them had as much education as I did, nor did they have as much experience.

In a sense, they all were enjoying what I had thought was the traditional way of promotions: hang around long enough and the company will take care of you. But they had been chosen and not me. So I wondered what it was about them that made them better.

I noticed a few minor things about their organizational skills and how they conducted themselves. For the most part, they followed policies and procedures to the letter. My theory is that they were chosen because they could be expected to behave in the manner prescribed by the company.

A Star-Child is Born

In the movie *2001: A Space Odyssey* there are two moments of universe shattering transformation. The first is when one of the ape-like primates, under the influence of the monolith, uses a bone to bludgeon an opponent at the waterhole. Life is never again the same for those ape-like primates.

The second is when the astronaut, Dave Bowmen, is transported to what seems to be a hotel†. and eventually transmogrifies into the Star-Child.

For me, I stopped being just a primate when I decided to try to improve my personal productivity and organization skills. I began to read books like David Allen's *Getting Things Done†* and Michael Lincnberger's *Master Your Workday Now!†*. They helped. I realized I could change my behaviors, get more done, and feel good about it.

As the mastery of those tools became second nature to me, I thought about ascending to leadership again. I started reading books on management. I did not, however, find a specific book that described in step-by-step fashion how to make yourself a god-like being with immense powers (i.e, a Star-Child).

I found books on how to manage people, how to be an effective supervisor, and how to manage teams. I found books on how to be an awesome leader or a kick-ass leader, but they were always targeted at existing leaders.

To me, being the guy on the bottom looking up, they all were a variation on: once you have your boot on their throat, here is how to keep the pressure on without killing them.

Learn How to Lead, Then Lead Yourself

The rest of this book will cover what leadership means on a personal level, especially if you are not yet a great leader and seeking inspiration.

We'll also discuss what leadership is not.

I'll soften you up with some jabs to the midsection to set a tone that will allow you to learn, change, and grow.

Then we'll assess what might already be your natural style of leadership. Even if we're not using those muscles, we probably have an attribute or two that will lend itself to leadership.

I'll present to you the well-known styles of leadership, and we'll break those down into simpler terms that will allow you to identify how you might learn one or more other styles.

And then we'll try to figure out a path that builds those skills and strengthens your abilities.

If You Can Lead Yourself, You Can Lead Others

Being a leader is as much about making the most of yourself as it is about making the most of others.

Stanley was certainly correct about one thing in that making yourself useful to others is considered the service style of leadership. But if you just focus on helping others with your service, you may never realize your leadership potential. Maybe he knew that all along, and I missed a crucial part of his advice.

I believe that finding a way to lead yourself to where you want to go, then you will have also learned how to lead others.

And if you want to ascend to one day become a Star-Child, consider that reading this book is a step on that journey. I'm not suggesting this book will get you there, but I'll do my damnedest to get you on the ship and launch you on the journey.

Attaining escape velocity requires help from others. I need that help as much as anyone, so don't be shy about asking.

5

LEARN EVERYTHING YOU NEED TO KNOW THE EASY WAY

"Leadership cannot really be taught. It can only be learned."

—Harold Geneen

There's Too Much For Me To Know

We all have moments of panic when faced with any new task. It's part of the brain's wiring to avoid risky behavior that might expend too much energy or put us in danger. Sometimes this panic is confused with actual danger when, in fact, there isn't anything wrong. The brain is just being the brain.

There absolutely is a lot to accomplish. You will have to commit to making a difference in your life. I used to think forming a habit took around 21 days? Why 21? Because that's what I always heard. Then I stumbled on an article about habit forming written by James Clear† and it turns out it can take from 50 to 250 days to form a lasting habit. That matched my experience.

A few years ago, my weight was becoming a problem for me. I had put on around 20 pounds of sympathy weight with my wife each time she had a baby. Carrying a few extra pounds is not a big deal. What I noticed about myself was that I was sneaking around eating sweets. I'd buy them and hide them in a closet, then sneak into that closet and eat in private. Just me and the chocolate.

It struck me that candy, especially chocolate, had taken control of my life.

I decided to give up chocolate for an entire year. At the time, I didn't know about the study cited in James Clear's article. I just picked a significant amount of time because I thought I had a significant problem, and that it would take a while to figure out.

That commitment made the difference.

After 75 days, I finally noticed that the cravings stopped, and I might go two days without even thinking about chocolate.

It occurred to me that if I could change that habit, I might be able to change others, as well.

I had a strong desire for starchy carbohydrates at that time in my life, and I had replaced a lot of my chocolate urges with bread. As a result, I really hadn't lost any weight by skipping chocolate.

I decided to skip starchy carbs, as well. And I decided to try this for a year to see if I could improve my weight. As with my earlier reasoning, I decided that I had taken 30 years to gain the weight, so it'd be fine to take one or more to lose it.

This resolve led to my transformational epiphany.

BOSS LESSONS

Commitment, Resolve and My Inner Dog Named Dimaggio

When my father retired from work, he had a dog, a little Bichon Frise named Peabody. My father took Peabody to McDonald's every morning for sausage. They stopped there most afternoons for ice cream, as well. The two of them were having a grand old time but, soon, the dog's weight doubled, and he looked like an over-stuffed pillow.

On a trip to the veterinarian, the doctor discovered that Peabody had diabetes and worried that he would not live much longer if he kept up this lifestyle.

My father was jolted back into reality, and began feeding Peabody a balanced, nutritional diet (no more McDonald's for the dog) and taking him on walks. It was an epiphany for my father.

Peabody lost weight, gained energy, and was more fun to be around. He was like a new dog.

It was six years later when I made my resolution to avoid chocolate and bread. These were not easy decisions for me, and as I mulled over my commitment, I thought of Peabody and how my father had nearly killed the poor brute by feeding him. And Peabody, knowing no better, was fine with eating everything offered.

My father should have known better than to share the bounty of America's abundance with a dog who was incapable of knowing that sausage and ice cream from McDonald's was not in his best interests.

And I realized that I was treating myself like I was a dog all these years, eating for pleasure, enjoying America's abundance, but I wasn't taking good care of myself. I should have known better than sneaking chocolate and devouring bread.

I realized I had to take better care of that dog (me). I realized I was not the sort of person to abuse dogs, so why the hell was I abusing me?

In short, my epiphany was to treat myself like a dog who needed better care than it had been given up to that point.

The first step was to give that dog a name: Dimaggio. (Why Dimaggio? Primarily because of the joke about the talking dog.)†

Using Dimaggio as a metaphor for my own well-being, I was able to begin a journey of self-improvement.

Because I was now caring for Dimaggio, rather than myself, I could convince my skittish brain not to panic over missing out on chocolate or bread.

Don't worry, you don't need an elaborate dog story of your own in order to gather the resolve necessary for a commitment to self improvement. In chapter 10, I discuss a much simpler way to create your own helpful self-image.

Meanwhile, take solace that there are three factors that work to your advantage in establishing the habits necessary for change.

Factor #1

You don't need to learn everything before you see the benefits of your new skill. You don't even need to learn a lot before you see the benefit.

When you first begin the habits of intentional living, there are small but noticeable changes in your brain patterns. You will start to feel better about yourself.

It's like the joy a baby feels when those first steps are taken into toddler-hood.

Factor #2

You can slip out of the new habit and return to them easily without any cause for concern or a reason to be upset.

Because you will be forming a habit, you'll eventually need 50-250 days of consistency to make it second nature. But unlike breaking bad habits, such as smoking, drinking, or binge-watching Gilmore Girls on Netflix, you aren't doing yourself additional harm when you backslide.

In fact, if you do miss a day and notice it, it's a moment to reflect on what you missed and how things went in the meantime. This allows you to adjust circumstances in your control to make tomorrow slightly better.

Factor #3

The very act of performing a ritual leads to improved enjoyment and happiness. As Eric Barker explains in this article (bakadesuyo.com†), *ritual* focuses the mind and allows us to more thoroughly enjoy the related event. This is just one of several brain-tricks you can employ, but it's the one we need right now.

So, when you do set aside a few minutes to plan how you will improve your leadership skills, you are setting yourself up to enjoy that activity.

The same thing happens when you reflect on how the day went: you give your mind a chance to be proud of itself and to know that at least some progress was made. It's also an excellent boost for the processing your brain requires during the night to make sense of what happened.

What Skills Do I Need to Develop?

If you're anxious to know what you need to know and haven't already skipped ahead, here is a summary of the skills you'll need to develop for leadership.

- 10 Leadership Styles (chapter 6)
- Emotional Intelligence (chapter 7)
- Character traits that help you excel (chapter 8)

Recall that we're not studying these to pass a test. We're taking baby-steps to gain mastery. If it takes two years that'll be fine because you will have been enjoying benefits all along. But it might just take a couple of months; i.e., your mileage may vary.

No More Excuses

It can be tempting to pretend to not care, and pretend you didn't know there was a better way, and go about living life just the way it is right now, running out the clock in a game you know you're not going to win.

But, that is only viable if you truly don't know there is a better way. You're reading this book, and I already told you there is a better way and that it ain't that hard to figure out.

I will indulge the thought with a story.

My father had a moment of despair when I was a kid. He was frustrated at his job, stressed about money, and was trying to figure out what to do next.

He told me about Max and Maxine, a couple he knew as a kid in the 1940s. They all lived in Brooklyn Acres, a housing project on Cleveland's south side. Max and Maxine were in their thirties, but they could have passed for being in their fifties. Their teeth were rotting, they had a variety of physical maladies brought upon by binge drinking, and their kids were out of control. They couldn't scrape two nickels together to ride the bus. But they always seemed happy. Max and Maxine were oblivious to their own problems, and always looked to have a good time.

My father related the story because he was aware that greater success and a better way to live was possible if only you could figure it out. In his moment of despair, he wondered if Max and Maxine didn't actually have the right attitude.

"Forget all this shit," he said, "and just go get drunk for the rest of my life."

His brain, wired for efficiency and wary of new challenges, was giving him an out. His own brain was offering him a chance to find a quiet place to ride out the storm, possibly for the rest of his life.

I'm Too Old to Change, and Nobody Listens to Me at Work Anyway

We all have moments of panic when faced with new challenges. But, by breaking down a challenge into baby-steps, and using a few mind-tricks of our own, we can slowly gain mastery over new things and improve our life.

Take Control of Your Destiny and Enjoy the Pursuit of Happiness

My father didn't have this book, but he did persevere and learned how to lead himself.

Among his challenges was education. He skipped college to join the Air Force during the Korean War.

When he returned to civilian life, he got a job, got married, and started making babies with my mother.

He took night classes for ten years, finally earning a degree in electrical engineering. When he retired after 40 years, he was one of the leading engineers at his company and designed the power substations for the largest building projects in the Cleveland area. He had taken charge of his career and his life and was satisfied with his accomplishments.

There are numerous other examples. My father's challenges were not particularly onerous, and neither were mine. But our brains are not very good at assessing the intensity of the challenges we face.

Our brains are quick to offer us an out. Our brains are constantly suggesting we skip this effort and go chill.

Our brains are that slacker friend who just wants to watch television and eat chips until it's time to take a nap.

Remind your brain it won't be so very bad, and that we're just going to take baby-steps until it's no big deal.

6

LAUNDRY LIST OF LEADERSHIP STYLES

"Leaders aren't born, they are made. And they are made just like anything else, through hard work."

—Vince Lombardi

A Key For Every Lock

Learning the different leadership styles will allow you to relax about learning the skills you need. You will hear attributes that you recognize as being your own, or of someone you admire. Also, you will probably recognize a few of the attributes in people you despise. (But let's focus on the positive.)

Leadership Styles Explained in Plain and Simple Terms

Study these to gain familiarity. Don't worry about memorizing anything, but be prepared to refer back to it as needed.

1. Autocratic—do what you're told just because

The autocratic style is awesome in a time of crisis, like multiple failed systems or a critical project that may not make its deadline.

The autocrat knows what processes should be used, knows what should be created or delivered at every step of that process, and has the confrontational fortitude to demand absolute compliance by everyone involved (even superiors of the organization). The autocrat wields power on behalf of the good of the organization.

To be more autocratic, you would first want to ensure you are comfortable with confrontation and conflict. Don't bother learning the processes and memorizing expected deliverables if you don't have the guts to demand them.

I was not comfortable with confrontation for decades. Two things helped me:

First, practicing my public speaking at my Toastmasters club loosened my tongue and improved my ability to think and speak when facing a crowd. It is amazing how difficult it can be to speak to a crowd when you are both the center of attention and expected to know what the hell you're talking about.

Second, my daily practice of meditation and regular practice of focus-oriented work keeps me engaged on finding a solution to a problem. Confronting anyone about a problem is easier if you focus on the solution rather than the drama.

Overly confrontational people have no problem telling you how badly you screwed up, and demanding to know why you screwed up. Once you've been dragged through the muck, then they'll worry about the solution.

If you don't want to be a party to that level of ugliness during a crisis, focus on the solution. Also, it will lead to a better solution sooner if the stress is minimized.

But just try to tell that to a confrontational autocrat.

2. Bureaucratic—do it the way it's supposed to be done

The bureaucratic style is handy if it's really important to follow policies and procedures, like if you're handling nuclear waste, transporting dangerous criminals, or methodically working your way through the Battlestar Galactica series and you don't want to misplace any of the DVDs.

But some large organizations, especially government agencies, become a bureaucracy. Those places may even lose touch with their purpose for existence, like in a Stanislaw Lem novel†.

To be more bureaucratic, you should focus on discovering and learning all the policies and procedures of your organization. I would encourage you to dig deep, because most people trapped in a true bureaucracy don't know all the rules.

If you always end up being the banker when playing Monopoly, or always bickered about the rules during a game of Scrabble, you might thrive as a bureaucrat.

Also, if you don't enjoy the confrontation involved while enforcing rules, the true bureaucrat sends an email about any infractions. No, wait—a true bureaucrat sends a memo about the infraction attached to an email, and in the email merely types, "See attached." Oh, and they CC the whole world.

MICKEY HADICK

3. Charismatic—Prince Charming stops by to ask a favor

The charismatic style is about utilizing personal influence to motivate the team. The charismatic leader might be quick with a smile, and friendly chat, then follows up with the ask. You're in such good humor from the visit that you hardly register the wink as the leader departs in a cloud of cologne.

That little disturbing vignette about Prince Charming is but one variation of the charismatic leader. There is also Cheerleader Chuck or Rah-Rah Rhonda, either one of whom will swamp your cubicle in enthusiasm while explaining what needs to get done.

Spiritual Sally is one who thinks the universe is in alignment at the moment so it's all going to be fine, but we need to change direction on the project in the meantime.

A true charismatic leader will share their version of enthused positivity with you, but doesn't really care whether or not you agree with the positivity as long as you get the work done.

I have painted this style in an unattractive shade of blah, but the aspect of influencing others with your personality is fundamental to leadership. All the styles depend somewhat on the personality of the leader, and this is leadership by personality.

If you don't think you have the type of personality to charm people into at least listening to what needs to be done, start now on improving your skills.

And if the schmooze is completely abhorrent to you, then take heart—there is a style of charisma that does not rely on strong extroversion, and it is probably the strongest form of charisma of all.

Engage your teammates and ask how they are doing. Listen carefully to what they say, especially if they are struggling at work or at home. Let them know you are concerned (if there is a problem) or gladdened (if all is well). Once they believe that you sincerely care about their circumstances, they will likely be interested in yours as well.

If you truly do not care about the circumstances of others, you will have a hard time developing leadership skills. Tyranny might work for you, but that is covered in an entirely different book.

4. Democratic—One person, one vote

The democratic style is easy to learn. You're giving a goodly amount of every decision over to your teammates. In its extreme, this is hardly leadership at all: you merely facilitate the wishes of the team. But in the extreme, this will not serve you or the team very well.

Some influence must be imparted by the leader when putting decisions to a vote, and some responsibility for the performance must be borne by that leader as well. If you manage a team and you grant them the power to vote on how work gets accomplished, it will be your fault when beer replaces coffee and pants become optional.

An off-shoot of this style is **participative**. Decisions are not put to the vote, but teammate opinions are sought and considered.

This is also easily learned, and if you've developed the empathy suggested under charismatic style, your teammates may believe that you care about what they think.

Both of these styles are cumbersome to maintain, and you may feel at times like a nursery school teacher who has lost control of the classroom.

5. Laissez-faire—do what you want

If we thought learning the democratic style was easy, laissez-faire puts it to shame. This French phrase means "leave it be." If you leave your team on their own, you have just adopted the Laissez-faire style.

It is vital that you learn when, and when not, to use this style. A good time to use it is when you're the boss but you're not the person who knows how to get things done, or everybody else is smarter or more specialized than you are. This scenario arises more often than most leaders realize.

As such a leader, you would do well to learn how to monitor progress without interfering. You probably should learn how to set your ego aside and direct all praise to the people doing the actual work.

If you decide on this style, but the team's performance suffers, you may have to kick into Autocrat to get the team back on track.

A variation of this style is **pace-setting**. If you are one of the smart people on the team getting things done, and you just happen to be in charge, you could let the others do their work with minimal direction, but you could also apply pressure to perform at a high level by generating your own output. Basically, you're showing them how it's done. (If you are one of these people then I think I speak for the rest of the world when I say, "we hate you.")

6. Relationship-Oriented—do the work and get a hug

The relationship-oriented style is a combination of the good parts of charisma style and participative style, and involves an extra helping of encouragement and concern.

If you are not a people person, this may be very difficult to learn. But, if you tend towards extroversion, you should be able to fake it.

Except, don't fake it, because you will come off as pandering and patronizing, and people hate that. Specifically, they'll hate you.

But, if you're ready to learn, start caring about others. If you lack empathy, try to figure out why.

If nothing else, put yourself in someone else's shoes (to borrow a phrase attributed to mothers everywhere) and see how you like it.

Assuming you have that figured out, and you are in fact using that style of leadership, you'll have to learn how to balance the concern for your teammates with the demand to produce. If you can summon your old friend the autocrat to apply occasional pressure, you may be able to make this work.

7. Servant—let me give you a hand with that

The servant style of leadership works best when you truly want to help others because you are concerned about them and seek no credit for yourself. It's a little bit like the relationship-oriented style, but you're not directly imposing your will.

In fact, this is a great style to use when you aren't in charge but you want to have an impact. Demonstrate your ability to get things done, your concern for others, and put the team's needs ahead of your own. This can be one hell of a triple-threat if you can pull it off.

If you offer to help because you want people to think you are helpful, but your heart is not truly in it, the façade won't last. You will be seen as either pandering or a sucker, and neither of those words describes a leader.

So, what is there to learn about being a servant?

Humility. You must learn to put others' interest before your own, without expectation of direct benefit. If you can manage that, then you can set a good example for others while demonstrating your usefulness.

Being a servant-style leader in an office environment does not mean you should do work for others but not take credit for the accomplishments. Take credit for your decision to serve, and make note of how it helped solve problems and created value for the company.

8. Task-Oriented—why are you doing it that way?

The task-oriented style pays attention to what everyone else is doing. And we mean really, really paying attention. The task-oriented leader pays more attention to what other people are doing than the people doing the thing are paying attention.

Task-oriented style is seen in high-output organizations like fast-food restaurants (flip those burgers), assembly lines (widgets and more widgets), and click bait websites (listicles of celebrity embarrassment). However, there is at least one awesome time when it is appreciated as a form of leadership: coaching.

When people are attempting to do something new— like learning to cook or to do something familiar but in an unfamiliar place—like work as a fry-cook on Venus —their brains may need help processing what is going on. They may need external help.

Enter the task-oriented leader. This leader must exhibit great observational skills, analytical skills, and patience in order to help. You must see what is going in an effort to do something, process what is working, identify what could be improved, and explain it to someone who is likely very frustrated.

To become this type of leader, you should work on the aforementioned skills of observation to notice each step in a task. You should practice analyzing those steps. How? Well, I'm glad you asked, as "analyze" is what I've done most of my life.

Analyzing processes boils down to clearly documenting the steps involved, understanding the purpose of each step, and identifying any risks, dependencies, or improvements for each of those. There's quite a lot to it, and it's very easy to gloss over things by making assumptions. But a good analyst gives equal attention to every step, and breaks them down to an atomic level.

Finally, structured thinking is necessary to clearly explain those steps and their related risks, dependencies, and improvements. A good way to improve that is to explain things in writing, and seek feedback about the clarity of the writing.

If you can put all of that together, and use those powers to assist those in need, you may be hailed as a great asset.

But if all you can bring yourself to do is tally up the outputs and criticize your team, no one will welcome your visits.

9. Transactional—it meets the output quota or it gets the hose

The transactional style is the tally-man who has come to tally me banana, now that daylight come and me wanna go home.

The proper environment for this is a place where everyone knows the rules up front—for a certain amount of productivity, a certain benefit will be granted. The leadership comes in the form of ensuring that all parties involved understand those rules, and that they are enforced equitably. Any breach of the rule will cause discontent and the team cohesion will deteriorate quickly.

Transactional style is definitely more a form of control because the focus is on consistent production levels rather than solving problems. The problem is usually the same. A certain production level may be set as a goal, but there is little vision involved. Creativity is not shared or sought. Just production.

So what is there to learn or develop for this style of leadership?

You must learn to set aside all bias when dealing with the team. Any hint of favoritism will lead to complaints and discontent faster than a broken toilet at a chili cook-off.

You must learn to control your emotions and limit empathy, focusing instead on cold-hearted evaluation of production numbers.

And if tempers flair, you must learn to be like Mr. Spock when surrounded by the Romulan fleet, gathering facts and using pure logic to recommend the most pragmatic course of action.

This style has its place, and the skills involved are useful in other situations, but it doesn't seem like fun to me. In fact, the only time Spock seemed to have fun was during mating season, and that seemed to be once every seven years.

10. Transformational—make better

The transformational style is based on a belief that everyone has a capacity to be better than they are, and maybe even to be amazing. In its extreme, transformational leaders are very upbeat, encouraging, and annoying.

The belief that others can accomplish more than they think they can has a dark side. Steve Jobs was considered transformational, but he was also reportedly demanding, abusive, and unwilling to compromise.

A kindhearted, pleasant-to-be-around transformational leader can be a joy in the workplace, and if you can figure out how to develop these skills, by all means do so, and make haste.

You'll need to work on your positive attitude. That may be a leap of faith at first, but studies have shown† that developing the habit of positive thinking changes the base outlook of a person and can increase their happiness (in self-reported surveys).

Also, happiness is just as contagious as gloom, so just bringing a smile to your team could be considered transformational leadership.

It helps, also, if you can develop your ability to generate ideas. This, too, is a skill you can improve by simply writing down ideas on a given topic in a focused manner. For example, pick something, anything, and write down ten ideas to make it better.

That could be ten ideas on how to make pencils better, or ten ideas on how to make vacationing with fam-

MICKEY HADICK

ily better. The ideas don't matter. Your ability to generate ideas and communicate, however, matters a lot. Practice that ability.

Bringing a variety of perspectives to problems always helps, so a transformational leader should read a variety of sources. Read news, read opinions, and research relevant topics. Follow your interests but also follow a few tangents.

Finally, learn to be comfortable with sharing ideas in public (or meetings with your team). If you are tongue-tied in front of people, all of your greatest ideas won't help solve a problem from inside your head. Join Toastmasters†, or practice talking to strangers at bars and coffee shops to get comfortable sharing those ideas.

7

NICE-TO-HAVES IN A LEADER'S PERSONALITY

"A leader takes people where they want to go. A great leader takes people where they don't necessarily want to go, but ought to be."

—Rosalynn Carter

To Lead, You May Need a Personality Adjustment

You might have all the leadership skills in the world spanning all the known leadership styles, and still not thrive as a leader. You may not even be able to lead yourself out of a wet paper bag, to mix a metaphor, if you don't have the personality for it.

But can the right personality be learned?

Of course. We attain personality throughout our lives. It's part of our very human ability to adapt to environments, especially challenging or dangerous places, like junior high. And whatever personality we had in junior high is likely jettisoned for the personality we need to survive high school, and then we do it again for college, and do it yet again at work.

Certainly, aspects of our personality persist, but as our circumstances in society and within our family change, other aspects of our personality are suppressed or emphasized in order to adapt and excel.

The easiest way to change your personality is to pick five people to hang around who are different from the people you hang around right now. That's because we become the average of the five people closest to us at any given time†. Change the people, change yourself.

So I Can Change—Now What?

Consider for a moment one tool which allows people to accomplish things consistently: mastery of their own emotions. Assuming a person does not have a mental condition that needs professional attention, mood swings dictated by emotions can be distracting at best, and left unchecked, can wreak havoc on their life.

Jealousy, envy, lust, fear, pride, and romantic infatuation are among the normal emotions we all experience on a given day. A business environment is often a competitive place where you will be asked to spend time with people you like, love, or hate. Allowing those emotions to control how you interact with them, and how you conduct yourself goes a long way in establishing your ability as a leader.

What was routine in junior high—emotional outbursts, petty jealousy, and bully tactics—should not be routine in a place of business. But I've seen such actions in employees, managers, and vice presidents. Some of my coworkers have harbored grudges for years over petty squabbles. Vice presidents, in my experience, gain control of their emotions quickly and focus on the challenges of the business.

Just Tell Me What to Do

I'm going to outline the four segments of emotional intelligence that you need to hone to be a strong leader. For a far more in-depth discussion, start with Leadership: The Power of Emotional Intelligence by Daniel Goleman†.

1. Self-Awareness—You recognize your own feelings, and gain perspective on how others perceive you

If you're not sure if you have this, then you probably don't. Being confident is not this. But this can give you confidence.

To get some, you may need some help on feedback from a trusted friend—ask them to tell you how you seem at any given moment. You may show a certain feeling (disappointment, anger, fear) on your face long before you consciously experience that feeling. Getting feedback quickly and consistently can help you connect the actual feeling with the body language expression of that feeling.

Feelings rush up from our subconscious and our physical body may express it before our conscious mind processes and acknowledges it.

This may seem like a lot to figure out, but it's well worth the effort. Even a little progress here will be noticed by others and it will help you see the world and yourself anew.

2. Self-Management—You don't lose control of yourself when things are getting weird, and can kick into another gear when needed

Stress can cloud our thinking or lead to rash judgments. And if the stress leads to an angry outburst at your teammates you will lose respect and demoralize them.

But if you can recognize your feelings and discuss them plainly and frankly ("This bad news is really bothering me. Are you upset? Do you have any ideas to improve the situation?") without accusing anyone of wrongdoing, you have a much better shot at making the best decision possible in the circumstances.

Also, if you are resilient when facing repeated challenges and can motivate yourself to keep solving problems, you will earn the respect of your teammates.

3. Empathy—You recognize others' feelings and share that emotion for their sake

Empathy starts with reading body language, as feelings show up physically even before the brain fully processes them. So pay attention.

You can then ask how someone is doing, and listen carefully. They may tell you directly what they're feeling, or they may not be able to until the feeling is processed into the consciousness.

But the fact that you asked, and that you care will usually be welcomed by that person. If you truly share in the feeling on their behalf, you will be making a real connection to someone, and building a level of trust that goes beyond teammate to trusted confidant or even friend.

4. Relationship Skills—You place value on the relationship and treat it with the appropriate respect

You don't have to be friends with your teammates, but you can still have a professional relationship that goes beyond common courtesy.

It is often inconvenient for teammates to pursue friendships outside of work, but taking lunch together, sharing a coffee break, or stopping for a drink after work can be very powerful in establishing a good working relationship. Demonstrating a sincere interest in strengthening the relationship is very flattering. For instance, making the effort to spend time with someone outside of work in order to get to know them would develop the relationship, even if no further bonds develop.

Taking lunch together is often done out of convenience or coincidence (i.e., bumping into someone at a restaurant). The deceptively simple act of scheduling a lunch or coffee together can be daunting because schedules often conflict, so when it works out, the value is recognized in having spent the time together.

8

OUGHT-TO-HAVES IN A LEADER'S CHARACTER

"Our chief want is someone who will inspire us to be what we know we could be."

—Ralph Waldo Emerson

How to Make Your Mother and Your Father Proud

The following attributes of a person's character can be learned by practicing them mindfully. But if you struggle with any of them, use self-compassion first, and don't think any less of yourself for lack of willpower. These are higher concepts of behavior that are dependent on multiple basic traits.

Also, many of these attributes are driven by your interest level in the task or the larger project. If you are bored by the work, or have no true stake in the success of the project, your drive may be lacking and your accountability for that success may be lackluster.

This is fine, but the trick is to convince yourself there is a great and exciting reason to work. If you can't think of sufficient reason on your own, I'll offer you a catch-all reason handed down over the generations from parent to child: "Doing things you don't like to do, but doing them well in spite of that, builds character."

There it is. If you wonder about your level of ability with these attributes of character, then working on something, and doing the work well, will ultimately build the character you desire.

Your parents will love you no matter what, but if you work towards developing these character traits, you will make them very proud.

1. Drive

The ability to get shit done is invaluable in every situation. Drive is the combination of resilience, stamina, and enthusiasm in the face of frustration and opposition.

Convincing yourself that doing the work is valuable, and achieving the result is the reward, is the best way to develop drive.

2. Accountability

Being responsible for results and caring enough about the progress made is accountability. It usually is brought up when things are not going to plan. The person keeping track of stuff and being brutally honest about the failings is likely the leader.

To develop accountability, you have to be comfortable with discussing disappointing results. If you're focused on the target, rather than looking for a celebration of what you've accomplished thus far, it will be appreciated from a management point of view.

The team will also appreciate that there is a leader willing to worry about how they will ever get things done.

3. Collaboration

Being a team player is the beginnings of collaboration, but if your participation ends at working for a common goal, you're not collaborative.

To collaborate is to find ways to help each other, and to complement each other's skills, while working together for a common goal.

Collaboration means sharing ideas, and listening to feedback, and adjusting efforts without feeling slighted by any critical suggestions.

It isn't always easy, but when you sincerely believe that working with your team in a collaborative manner produces the best results, your teammates will trust you, and the collaboration will become easier.

4. Humility

As a leader, you needn't be humble all the time, but I think it's good to know when you ought to show some humility. Especially if you are making an effort to be collaborative, don't throw all that away by being cocky or taking credit.

If you need help in playing your humility card from whatever hand you've been dealt, just try to recall that we all make mistakes and we all need help. If you did anything correct today, someone showed you how at some point in your life, even if it was your mother teaching you how to wipe your butt.

5. Justice

A sense of fair play and honesty are critical to being trusted. If you distribute the work, the rewards, or the punishments associated with team efforts unjustly, the backlash from teammates will be immediate and vicious.

I believe justice and humility go hand-in-hand. So be gentle when correcting mistakes, because we all make them on a regular basis.

Be generous with pointing out the successful efforts of others, as they will appreciate it, and it will likely inspire them to live up to your high praise.

6. Courage

There will be times when giving up seems the smartest thing to do. But if you are convinced that your project can succeed, or if you have given your word that will complete a task, continuing when conflict and confrontation have arisen will be a sign of courage.

The cowardly lion in *The Wizard of Oz* went on a long journey to convince himself that he was courageous. All of us have been on a long journey already ourselves, but we still may need reminding that we have courage within us.

If you get out of bed and get yourself to work in the morning, that is a form of courage. If you care for your family, or show concern for neighbors or friends, that is another form of courage.

When faced with great opposition, remind yourself of your convictions. What are you working to achieve? Who stands to benefit when you succeed. How much will be lost if you turn away out of fear?

7. Integrity

If you have at least a little bit of each of the previous attributes of character, you likely have a reputation of integrity.

MICKEY HADICK

But what if you don't? What should you do to demonstrate and strengthen your integrity?

Be trustworthy with your teammates' time, talents, and possessions. Show up on time for meetings, allow teammates with a particular skill to use those talents to full effect, and don't take anybody's lunch out of the office refrigerator.

Be reliable for what you say you can do, and what you promise to figure out when you know you can't do it otherwise. A team needs every member to do their share as they say or have been asked to do. Those who would lead must be relied upon to do all that they can.

9

JOE SCHMOE AND AUNT FLO BECOME CEO

"Do not wait on a leader. Look in the mirror, it's you!"

—Katherine Miracle

We All Have Within Us the Ability to Lead

Humans are social animals, and leadership emerges in our social groups naturally. There are those that will assert themselves as a leader without consciously making the decision. Their tone of voice, word choices, and body language impose their presence on others in the group, vying for attention and, ultimately, leadership.

An equally natural phenomenon is that others in the same group might also vie for leadership, but then stop when they consciously or unconsciously decline to challenge with their tone of voice, word choices, or body language.

Still others in the same group might not ever challenge for leadership. Their natural state is to find contentment in following others.

So does that mean some humans are incapable of leadership?

I don't think so. I think those who choose not to challenge for leadership in social situations have the ability, but that something keeps them from asserting themselves.

But what?

Fear and Shame

Fear and shame are the most debilitating of emotions. Fear of the unknown keeps us out of dark places. Shame, or the fear of shame, stops us from taking risks because we are afraid of embarrassment and ridicule.

And it is also true that acting as a leader draws attention. Those we lead will scrutinize our words, our posture, and our actions. We may think that it is necessary to be always correct if we are to lead. But leaders are still human. That's right, being perfect is not a requirement for being a leader.

You needn't be proud of your mistakes, but neither do you need to be ashamed of them, except for one: to step down from leadership out of fear of being shamed.

The ridicule directed at leaders is normal. In fact, that's one of the indicators that you truly are a leader, some of your followers will ridicule your actions. In a related note, those who ridicule leaders may be itching to lead themselves.

We All Play Follow the Leader

Without this willingness to follow, we would hardly talk, probably wouldn't get along, and humans would still be just one of various animals wandering across the wilderness in search of a carcass to steal from a real predator.

The fear and shame that prevents us from acting as a leader also pressures us to act like those around us so that we don't draw undue attention.

The fact that we are following the lead of our neighbors means that leadership can still be active far from the formal leadership of your group, like a president or senator

The couple next door, Joe Schmoe and Aunt Flo, are just as likely to be leaders as the couple next to them.

So what keeps Joe Schmoe and Aunt Flo from being CEOs?

Be CEO of Your Own Life

If Joe Schmoe and Aunt Flo next door intentionally decide to take charge of their life, and direct the course of events that will become their future, they will have appointed themselves CEOs of Their Own Lives.

You don't have to run a corporation to be a CEO, you just have to take charge of your own life.

It Happens to the Best of Us

When I was in college, I fantasized about running a large corporation. I had gotten into a pretty good school, and I was studying a pretty tough curriculum (Computer Engineering). So, I thought, I was pretty smart. I figured a smart guy like me should be able to run a company someday.

That turned out to be fanciful thinking because even though I learned how to design and program a computer, I never developed my leadership skills.

In fact, I went from job to job, not quite ever sure why I wasn't being promoted, in spite of working very hard and getting some great work done for my clients.

What was even more telling, I wasn't taking care of my health. I put on weight, became inactive, and stopped caring about the consequences because I became convinced I was not meant for leadership. I started to question if I was worthy of a promotion because it hadn't worked out that way.

I Had to Learn to Lead Myself

I mentioned in chapter 5 that I had an epiphany resulting in me taking charge of my own life. At that moment, I had taken a new job and was dreaming that, this time, it would lead to promotions and success. I was 41 years old, and I thought things would work out this time. But I was really hoping that someone would notice my talent and make things happen for me.

I was looking for the right leader to serve, as Stan the Man had taught me twenty years earlier, and hoping that some leader would take care of me.

But my epiphany about my health (Dimaggio, my inner-dog) allowed me to realize I needed to take care of all aspects of my destiny.

This all didn't happen at once. It was a learning process that began with my health, and then reached into my state of happiness, and has finally branched into my professional life.

I didn't know what I was getting myself into but, over time, I came to know that I was the only person for the job. Nobody else, I realized, was going to make me any better than I was.

Learning to Walk All Over Again

At the time of the epiphany, I started reading self-help books. There were a lot I studied, and there have

BOSS LESSONS

been tons more written since. You should read one or two yourself, just as you are reading this.

Why not just this one?

It took your brain a couple of years to learn how to walk, run, and skip. Since that time, you've spent 20 or 30 years learning about yourself and how the world works. Now you're learning that you can develop leadership skills and, with intentional living, transform your life. It will take longer than the time it takes to read this book to master those skills.

In fact, because of your brain's built-in desire to keep things simple, it will resist this learning. It will want to ignore your command to change and will seek moments to suggest going back to however things were before.

You will have to read this book over again, or read other books to enforce the idea that you can change the way you perceive yourself in the world, and ultimately transform your life.

Some people need the confidence boost of an outside support group. There are personal development organizations that are designed to help you improve your self confidence, assertiveness, and leadership skills. Dale Carnegie† offers training and coaching in small group settings. I haven't personally attended that training, but I've heard good things.

But I did join a Toastmasters† club around the time of my epiphany. Toastmasters is a public speaking group that offers leadership training through participation in group activities in a supportive environment. It is also a lot of fun. You are encouraged to get up in front of the group and deliver speeches. In my ten years as a member, I've seen dozens of people overcome fear of public speaking, and even thrive at the front of the room. There is likely a club meeting near you†.

Back to Reading

Here are some great books that helped me along my way. I hope they help you too:

- The Obstacle Is the Way: The Timeless Art of Turning Trials into Triumph by Ryan Holliday
- Maximize Your Quality of Life by Tom Matt
- Think and Grow Rich: The Landmark Bestseller —Now Revised and Updated for the 21st Century by Napoleon Hill (an oldie but a goodie)
- The Science of Hitting by Ted Williams (how to hit Major League pitchers)
- The Tools: 5 Tools to Help You Find Courage, Creativity, and Willpower,—and Inspire You to Live Life in Forward Motion by Phil Stutz and Barry Michels

Your Call to Action

I opened this chapter by arguing that all of us has the ability to lead. But factors in us and outside of us will conspire to suppress that ability.

You owe it to yourself to find a way to develop your ability to lead.

Persist, and you will succeed. Teach your mind to overcome the resistance holding you back. You will master these leadership skills and you will begin to lead an intentional, and fulfilling life. Even if you only lead yourself, your life will be better because of it.

That's what I'm doing now, and that's why I'm sharing what I learned.

10

WHAT'S DIFFERENT THAT DOESN'T COME DOWN TO BOSSES BEING BOSSY?

"If you don't understand that you work for your mislabeled 'subordinates,' then you know nothing of leadership. You know only tyranny."

—Dee Hock

Who Your Boss Is

We all have bosses in one form or another. If you're a cubicle-dweller like me, you probably have three bosses at any given moment. If you're a manager, then you have a director or vice president as your boss. Even the CEO reports to the board and the shareholders.

What we all want is a boss who treats us fairly and with compassion.

Also, we want a boss who has a clue about what's going on—that's part of the motivation for this book: to remind you that if your boss is clueless, you'd better be ready to lead yourself so that you can get your work done.

But, to lead an intentional life you must not be a jerk to yourself. And you sure as heck better not plan on being a jerk to other people if you do end up as a boss.

So how do we stop you from turning into just another butthead boss, capable of stinking up the workplace just by opening his mouth to speak?

My Inner-dog

When I had my epiphany and decided to improve my life, I realized I wasn't taking good enough care of myself. I realized that I was treating myself like a dog I hated, and abusing that dog (me) to the point of an early death.

I realized I had to take better care of that dog (me). I realized I was not the sort of person to abuse dogs, so why the hell was I abusing me?

As I mentioned back in chapter 5, the first step was to give that dog a name: Dimaggio. (I chose that name because of the joke about the talking dog†).

Using Dimaggio as a metaphor for my own well-being, I was able to begin a journey of self-improvement.

This worked for me, but I learned in my continuing self-help education that I had stumbled on a classic philosophical question about the concept of self. However, I made an eensy, teensy mistake.

In a Psychology Today article†, Dr. Stephen Diamond discussed how the psychiatrist C.G. Jung argued that the human subconscious harbors an image of the self that embodies the darkest impulses of human emotions, like lust, anger, and jealousy, that have been suppressed by the individual in an attempt to conform to society's expectations. We recognize that a particular urge will heap shame upon us if we act on the urge, and so instead we hide it in our subconscious.

This collection of urges which we deny expression becomes our shadow-self. Because these repressed urges all have a personal connection to our desires, the shadow-self is a version of our conscious self. If we met our shadow on the street, we would recognize much of what we saw, but there might be a goatee on our face, a leather vest on our torso, and probably a bad-ass tattoo on our chest.

Jung constructed this model of a shadow-self, at first, to help explain the source of evil in our hearts, especially extreme evil in murderous leaders. But it also helps explain the source of inspired creativity many of us exhibit.

The shadow-self is built of morally reprehensible urges, but it also is built of normal tendencies that were inappropriate at the time and had to be suppressed. For instance, as a child, we might want to be a ballet dancer, or a professional baseball player, or a rock star. Our parents, however supportive they may be, may talk us out of those dreams for our future. And so the urge to dance, play, or rock it out becomes part of our shadow-self.

In fact, for those of us with normal upbringings, relatively free of violence danger, we may dream about a lot of fun, creative pursuits that become impractical to achieve as our talent, training, and opportunities develop. Even as we go from high school to college, we might change an initial dream of becoming a medical doctor into a bachelor's in psychology. Instead of working to save lives in a hospital, we might sell software to insurance companies. Selling software is nothing to be ashamed of. But the dream of being a doctor becomes one more regressed urged added to our shadow-self.

My Shadow-Self

My confusion in approaching my shadow-self was to think of it as a dog. That dog, Dimaggio, needed care, and helping Dimaggio started me on a path of improvement. But that dog did not inform me of all my repressed dreams and urges.

A more useful version of your shadow-self is the child who was told to quit dreaming of dancing, singing, or playing all their life. The child who is told to forget about being president, or to give up their wish to be a movie star feels the sting of shame.

My inner child wanted to act in plays and tell jokes, but I was told that those things are silly, and not what real men should do. And my inner child wanted to make books and tell stories, but was instead told to study math and science.

Your Shadow-Self

The inner child in your mind is you at an early age before becoming aware of the many disappointments life has to offer. As we grow older, that inner child falls farther and farther in shadow, quietly waiting, hoping someone will come and take care of them.

But instead, we heap abuse and neglect upon our shadow- self. When we don't take care of ourselves, we quietly hurt our shadow-self. And when we find ourselves deeply unhappy and dissatisfied with how our lives are going, it's time to look inside and figure out what our shadow-self wanted out of life that has not materialized.

How to Care for Your Shadow-Self

If there is anything you always wanted to do but never got around to do it, or decided it was just a silly dream not worth pursuing, that's the sort of thing you absolutely must do to care for your shadow-self.

For me, it was taking writing seriously. Eating better, exercise, and reading were things I needed to do, as well. Those were things that restored my strength and allowed me to write better, more regularly, and to begin to express my creativity, just as my shadow-self had always wanted to do.

You will have to take a moment to check on your shadow-self, recall the things you always wanted to do, and make sure you have been, or are willing to start caring for that inner child.

The Kid's Doing Better Than Me—So What?

Learning to care of your shadow-self is a lesson in compassionate leadership. It's the butthead boss who will abuse or neglect that child for the sake of some accomplishment the child does not care about. We do not want to learn to be a butthead boss.

If you learn to properly care and feed your shadow-self, you will thrive like never before. People will notice the improvement. You may even inspire them to act more like you do.

If you can inspire people, then you can transform their work and their lives. And that will make you a transformational leader.

But it all starts with yourself.

Leading Passively

We humans are social animals. We don't exactly herd, but we don't live our lives in isolation. We notice what others do, and we tend to mimic them. Did you ever reach for a cookie when you saw someone else grab one from the bag? Did you start with fear when someone near you made a sudden movement? Did you ever do the wave at a stadium because of the other 80,000 doing the wave?

Sometimes the urge behind the mimicry is competitive jealousy, as in grabbing a cookie before they are all eaten by someone else. But mimicry is also caused by empathy and compassion, such as when a person yawns, and you yawn as well. Or if you laugh in sympathy at another person's nervous, awkward laugh. We are sharing that moment with the other person.

In short, we tend to follow the lead of those around us. We may not realize it, but people around us are following our lead as well. It happens all the time, every single day, but at an almost imperceptible level.

What if we consciously think about our actions and how they affect those around us? What if we think about our own reactions to what we see happening around us, and decide for ourselves whether or not to follow someone's lead.

If we have learned how to care for our shadow-self, and act accordingly, it will be much easier to decide how to react to what is going on in the world, especially in our business world.

And if those around you see how you act, and recognize that you are thriving, they will mimic you and follow your lead.

Chase Butthead Boss Away

If years of low-budget office comedies have taught us one thing, the butthead boss can't be killed. The butthead emerges from the organizational dysfunction time and again.

People become butthead bosses when they are placed in a leadership role without a full grasp of the skills needed. They usually have abused their shadow selves so thoroughly that now they uncontrollably abuse the people around them.

You may not be able to escape butthead bosses, but you don't have to let him destroy you (even as he stinks up your cubicle with a useless motivational speech).

Care for yourself, care for your shadow-self, and let your ability to thrive inspire and lead others.

And then use the leadership skills you develop to exert influence.

Key Action Items

- Recognize the moments in our life when we are subconsciously following someone's lead.
- Look for the moments when, conversely, others might be following us, as well.
- Begin to think of our actions and reactions — which are conscious, and which are social instincts?
- Incorporate an evaluation of those actions and reactions — is it what we want to do because it will lead us to our goals and objectives?
- Combine this with the sincere desire to improve your life (or family, or job) and those around you will recognize that following your lead will help make things better.

If you can incorporate those simple moments of reflection and consideration into our day-to-day lives, you have taken a major step toward leadership.

And the first person to benefit from that leadership is you. You are now taking the first steps on whatever path you wish to follow.

11

INSPIRE FOLLOWERS RATHER THAN MANIPULATE THE MEEK

"You manage things; you lead people."

—Grace Murray Hopper, U.S. Navy Rear Admiral

Be a Leader Without Falling Into the Trap of Being a Boss

The conflict averse may want to remove all possibilities of becoming what they hate: a pushy, obnoxious butthead of a boss. You may want to pledge yourself to a lifetime of servitude, never seeking out a management position, or any sort of responsibility that calls for leadership.

I frequently encounter people at the businesses where I work who were once in management, and have happily been demoted, never again to apply for a promotion involving leadership.

How do I know this about their employment history? It's because those people share the fact that they used to be a boss, but they'll never do that again. It was traumatic, and has scarred their psyche into never taking that risk again.

I Don't Want to Become a Butthead Boss

By first nurturing your shadow-self, and learning to care for yourself, you strengthen your ability to lead while learning to love yourself at the same time.

As you begin to thrive and improve your good habits, your outlook on the challenges you face will improve as well. You will learn to do things for yourself without having to suffer.

To switch to a fitness metaphor, you are strengthening the core of your leadership. And any trainer worth the sweat on their brow will tell you that strengthening your core is the key to achieving great things in fitness.

But when you resort to negative self-talk and scold yourself for being weak in order to force yourself to exercise, you are practicing self-loathing. And if you practice self-loathing, you will strengthen your self-loathing muscles.

Similarly, you can't nurture your shadow-self by berating yourself about having failed at things before. Only by practicing self-compassion can you nurture your shadow-self.

By self-compassion, I mean forgiving yourself for not having pursued you childhood dreams. And of course, you should. First of all, when you are a child, most of the circumstances of your life are beyond your control. And later, once you took on adult responsibilities, you may not have known about your shadow-self or how it impacted your conscious decisions.

I was 43 when I finally began to realize I could take control of my life. It was another two years before I learned about my shadow-self, and began to nurture that long-abused child.

The best way to learn to be a great leader is to learn how to care for your needs and to arrange things for yourself so that you inspire yourself to achieve. You must practice self-compassion that cares for your shadow-self.

Transformational Leadership Can be Learned

As you improve your own situation, and build the habits of leadership, you will begin to transform your own life. You are gaining mastery over yourself, and opening up the possibilities of an intentional life.

And you may begin to notice how others around you are doing the same for themselves.

I used to be convinced that some people were just born to be happy, successful, and (ultimately) lucky. For some people it was better genes, or a faster metabolism, or a smarter brain. I used this as an excuse for not taking care of myself.

Once I realized it was possible to care for yourself, I noticed people around me thriving, and I learned as much as I could from them on how to do the same for myself.

The People Near Me Who Thrived

This is mostly about the leadership of small things, but I began to exercise more regularly a few years ago when two different neighbors led me by their example. The first neighbor, I'll call her Yvonne, was an avid runner. She sat in the cubicle next to mine at work, and we chatted about running. I had done just a bit of running in the past, but gave it up, convinced I wasn't built for it.

There certainly are body types that are more likely to excel at running, but there is no reason that any person capable of walking can't also enjoy the potential benefits of jogging or running.

Yvonne extolled running because of how good it made her feel, and how the effects lingered. If she missed a day out of her routine, she noticed it.

I was inspired by her love for that feeling, and how happy she was on the days that she had gone for a run.

I decided to try it myself. Soon I was telling her of my running habit, and we compared notes about accomplishments. She encouraged me with assurances that things would get better if I kept at it. That started me on a path that would radically improve my life. And never once did she admonish me, taunt me, or bully me.

Yvonne exhibited sincere and authentic pleasure in her habit of running, and I followed her lead. I wasn't even aware of how it happened at the time. I merely decided to start running, and then kept at it because we chatted about it at work. Only much later, as I tried to understand how this change happened, I realized it was her leadership that changed my life.

The change in my life accelerated when my next door neighbor Tom also began exercising. He had not been in great shape, but he began lifting weights, running, and doing various body-weight exercises. He was very excited about this, and was studying to become a certified trainer, eventually he wrote a book† about his experience.

I saw his enthusiasm and intense pleasure sparked by his accomplishments in the gym. He was a bit on the obsessive side of regularity, but he inspired me to stay with it. Our conversations about exercise were also about how important nutrition is, and as he improved his eating habits, mine improved as well.

I saw his transformation and learned from it.

This experience improved my physical well-being, but what about my emotions? What about my shadow-self?

But Do I Deserve to Be Happy?

I had another friend at work, I'll call her Lina, who seemed happier than everybody else. Not that things always worked out for her. She had a stressful job, two small children at home, and her husband also had a demanding job. She worked for a total butthead. There were plenty of reasons for her to be frustrated with life. I've encountered dozens of people who complained about far less. But she shrugged off the challenges and decided to be happy.

She had an amazing capacity to keep perspective on what mattered in her life. If the work she did at her job was never enough to satisfy her boss, then she knew her family's well-being was primary, and that her relationship with friends strengthened her shadow-self.

She made a point to schedule dates with her daughters, husband, and her girlfriends from college. It required extra effort and planning on her part, but it was the best way she knew of to take care of her relationships in life. She was nurturing her shadow-self by taking care of those relationships.

I commented to Lina about her efforts. I jokingly said I was jealous, but also that I didn't think I deserved to be that happy. That the things that made me happy were beyond my control.

Lina was deeply concerned that I would believe, even for a moment, that I did not deserve to be happy. She offered me some ideas to convince me that I was worthy of happiness.

I learned from her that each of us deserves to be happy (even if it doesn't always work out or come easily) and that we owe it to ourselves and each other to do what we can to make happiness attainable. This was before The Happiness Project† was around, and so, to me, her ideas were groundbreaking.

You Will be the First Beneficiary of Your Leadership

The one thing you need to do that inspires confidence and motivates people is to thrive at what you do.

Thriving does not simply mean you seem happy with your lot in life.

Thriving is not simply being cheerful when you arrive at your job.

Thriving does not simply mean doing lots of work without complaint.

Thriving is all of those things and more. (Yes, even doing lots of work.)

Thriving is facing the challenges you face with confidence that they can be overcome or avoided as needed, and that, whatever the solution, your shadow-self will be cared for, and the lessons you learn will go towards improving your life in a way that you've decided is right for you.

The sooner you begin to practice your craft, the sooner you will enjoy the benefit. As others notice your change and the improvements you enjoy, you will gain respect and authority. You will exert influence and you will be thanked for it.

So how do we get on with it and begin these lessons in leadership?

Prescription

1. Pick a specific area in your life to improve, such as fitness, eating habits, sleep, or education. (NOTE: an ideal area to improve is one related to the care of your shadow-self.)
2. Verify the leadership style most likely to be effective for your personality (transformational is a great one if you aren't sure)
3. Establish the habit of planning the day each morning — in a span of five minutes — how you will lead yourself in the specific area
4. Document the day's plan in a journal. (Recall that I suggested a dedicated planner, such as the SELF journal, but any piece of paper will do the trick.)
5. Work towards the specific improvements during the day.
6. Review and adjust the plan around mid-day.
7. At the end of the day, review your results, and make note of how you could improve, and how your leadership (of yourself) worked or did not work.
8. Congratulate yourself for working on your leadership and on improving a specific area of your life.

Optionally, reward yourself. If you've made the effort to plan something to improve, you check your progress, and accomplish your goal for the day (or week) giving yourself some reward adds ritual to the exercise.

The ritualized act of rewarding or congratulating yourself is not gratuitous. It is a technique for establishing habits, and also caring for your shadow-self. This has a powerful effect when established as a habit, and will lead to the authentic and sincere joy of accomplishment. When you reinforce a good habit with positive reflection, it strengthens your subconscious desire to experience it again.

Now make all haste and begin to practice, even as I write more about developing your leadership skills.

12

HOW TO LEAD
A SPECIFIC PERSON

"Example is not the main thing in influencing others; it is the only thing."

—Albert Schweitzer

How to Increase Your Ability to Lead Specific Individuals

The challenge of leading can be daunting. If you've never worked on your leadership skills you may always be as frightened as a virgin on their wedding night. And if, in the past, you've done nothing more than rely on the authority of your appointed position, you may have hidden behind a bully's pulpit to get things done.

Either way, it probably wasn't very much fun.

We have already reviewed some leadership styles that may help, but how do you know which to choose for any given situation?

Who Wants to Follow Someone Like Me, Anyway?

I assumed my first business leadership roles before I had begun to care about myself. I was fourteen years into my career and working for a company called Sequoia Services (later bought by Analysts International; and now, who knows?). We provided talent for technology projects, and I was assigned to manage a project to design and develop software for the Michigan Supreme Court. I was the only person from my company on the project.

The implementation team was a mixed bag. They were chosen by the executive sponsor at the Supreme Court, and each one was completely beyond the reach of any formal employment control wielded by me. That is, half of them worked for the Supreme Court, and the other half were there on a pre-existing contract. Most of them were older and more experienced than I was. Nobody had any reason to listen to anything I said.

Like a virgin on my wedding night, I was shy, clumsy and not sure how to even ask for what I wanted done. If I'd had any authority to be a bully, I likely would have resorted to that out of cowardice.

Over the ensuing months, we muddled along, learning to get things done together, but nobody really enjoyed it. We certainly weren't thriving.

My position was "de-funded"" (in the parlance of contract work) and I was sent packing before completing my work.

If You Can Inspire Yourself to do Something Good, Then You Can Inspire Anyone

The greatest hurdle on the path to leadership is convincing yourself that you are worthy enough to be followed.

People who notice that you care about yourself enough to try to make things better will likely be receptive to your leadership. If you're thriving, and they notice and admire your efforts, they may crave similar attention.

The solution is to then care about another person as if they were as important to you as your shadow-self. Find out what that other person needs. Can you see their shadow-self? Connect their needs to the needs of the project (whatever the work is) and then together take steps to fulfill their needs while accomplishing the work at hand.

A Team is a Team is a Team

A team of workers is like a youth sports team—they dress like professionals, but at heart they are just a bunch of kids. I say that as a reminder to be compassionate about their needs, not to be condescending or even cavalier about co-workers and their quirks or weaknesses.

How to Lead a Specific Person, Whether Part of a Team or Just by Themselves

1. Begin by caring about the other person's problem.
2. Allow your authentic and sincere concern to show.
3. Search for an answer (not necessarily the answer) to improve the situation.
4. Reflect on how your leadership style affects their performance.
5. Adjust your style as needed.

One More Word About the Parenting Side of Leadership

Being a leader at a business is all too often like being a parent. The nice part of business is that you can usually walk away from your problems at the end of the work day. In fact, it helps to ignore work problems for awhile.

I've noticed that people often have a juvenile side that is revealed during times of stress or frustration at work. It's not that they lack maturity, although some may, rather, they may not have taken adequate care of their shadow selves, and the tantrum you see at work is likely a tantrum being thrown within.

Parenting leadership—which is primarily transformational style—is highly effective at such times.

13

WHAT IF I'M SURROUNDED BY BUTTHEAD BOSSES?

"You have to look at leadership through the eyes of the followers and you have to live the message. What I have learned is that people become motivated when you guide them to the source of their own power and when you make heroes out of employees who personify what you want to see in the organization."

—Anita Roddick

We Have Too Many Leaders Who Don't Know Their Ass From Third Base

Poor leadership, like any bad idea, can be infectious and spread throughout an organization. Tragically, bad ideas can infect entire countries and plummet nations into war.

In his book Give and Take†, author Adam Grant explains how selfish, exploitative behavior spreads from person to person, especially if their organization rewards that behavior even slightly.

He also explains how the opposite, sharing behaviors, can spread. They can even counteract the negativity and help change the company culture.

If you find yourself surrounded by buttheads, you may be able to resist their poor leadership ideas and start something good. That is, you can demonstrate strong leadership and inspire others.

Even if the company is controlled by an unadulterated butthead boss, you may be able to build a life raft of good leadership and stay afloat, at least long enough to find a safe island of refuge. By that I mean find others in the company who share your frustration, try to accomplish needed work with their help, and offer your services to them to ease the frustration. You will create a network of like-minded people from whom you can draw inspiration. And you can strengthen your resolve to survive the butthead boss.

I can attest to this happening.

Hey, Is That Greener Grass I See?

Almost 20 years ago, when I worked for Unisys in relative obscurity, and before I understood the value of leadership and intentional living, I heard about a local company that was making money and hiring technical people. I mistakenly thought I could recognize a real opportunity when I saw one, and interviewed for a job.

The company was a smaller, nimbler version of Unisys, and provided computer networking solutions to the State of Michigan and local government agencies in mid-Michigan. The interview went well and I was invited back for a second interview with the company's president.

When I returned, much had changed. A new owner had bought the company and swept in to take charge, causing a dispute over operational control. Fourteen of their technical experts quit and walked out, leaving an immediate need for systems engineers. Several administrative and management people left, as well.

The good news was that I was offered a much better job than what I had originally hoped to land. At least I thought it was good news.

I Wonder Why All Those Smart Guys Quit?

The exodus of technical talent might have been a great challenge, but the company still held one lucrative contract to supply computer equipment and services. They had this money guaranteed if they could just find the engineers to install and support it.

I should have wondered what could be so awful about the guy who had jumped to the front of this parade, but I was too excited about the new gig.

What I learned over the next four months is that the new leader was focused purely on the profitability of their big contract, and cared little for the satisfaction and care provided to the customer.

He cared nothing for the careers, training, and well-being of the people he hired to replace the mutineers, and even less for the faithful who had not walked out.

Managers demanded work, executives slashed benefits, and customer complaints were ignored.

Icebergs Spotted Ahead

What I've described about the job seems like it would have been an obvious crisis, but all seemed well from the deck of the ship. The company still had the contract, the customer paid the invoices, and the employees were being paid their wages. It wasn't like the boat had struck something and was listing to port as water poured in below.

What I was slow to realize was the dangerous currents beneath the surface of the water that slowed progress. We all felt frustrated, and we noticed when tempers flared as various problems were left without a viable solution.

In response, I found myself gravitating to one of the five salespersons, a woman who had a knack for engaging customers and solving their problems by selling them our products and services.

She wasn't in it for the money. Instead, she embodied what I now understand to be a **servant**-style of leadership, finding ways to help others in order to get the needed work done.

She listened with compassion to the customer's problems, and worked very hard to find the combination of tools and talent to help them out.

She sought out help from the technical experts for the solution, but she didn't demand it like an autocrat, or trick us with charisma. Instead she showed concern for our workload, offered to help if needed, and asked for the solution with sincere empathy for our customer.

I was happy to help out, and gave extra energy to find the solution for her.

The leadership she provided was like a life raft on a sinking ship.

And by the way, in spite of not being in it for the money, she was the leading salesperson on staff. Her approach to helping potential customers led to closing lucrative deals.

Great. Now what?

1. Recognize when your manager is not your leader, then seek out or provide the needed leadership.
2. Embrace the fact that if your manager is a bossy tyrant, you may be better off without this job.
3. Do not confront the bossy tyrant about this problem. You won't solve that problem, and you will likely create a bigger problem instead.
4. Identify the missing leadership, and look for it elsewhere, or consider providing it yourself.
5. Lead yourself and any others that will follow in the direction you need to go. Try to solve the problems that matter to the company first. Then work on the problem with your boss.
6. Offer to provide that leadership to your team as a service to your boss.

Back On the Boat

It was a difficult and frustrating time at that formerly nimble upstart, and the team became fractious. Over the next few months, squabbling, arguing, and complaining became a normal daily reality.

Those of us who recognized the need for refuge found each other, and worked to get things done in spite of the growing dysfunction.

I might have jumped ship immediately, but I needed to earn money. By finding like-minded individuals and caring about each other, we created a place of temporary refuge. With that, I was able to last long enough to find a job with another company where the culture and leadership values made me feel welcome and safe.

The Set of The Sails

I always thought that sail boats moved because the sails caught the breeze, and the boat was pushed along by the wind. Although that is one way to sail, you are more like a kite at that point. Being shoved by the wind, you are at the mercy of that wind, and have little control over your destination.

A sail works best when it angles into the wind. As a sail fills with air, it takes the shape of a wing, and the difference in air pressure propels the boat into the wind. That is why sail boats will tack at forty-five degree angles into the wind. You cannot take on a headwind directly, but you can let the force of that wind pull you closer in that direction rather than being pushed away.

By developing your skills, you can navigate dangerous waters on your own terms. Do not remain at the mercy of the wind.

14

THE MOST IMPORTANT THING A LEADER CAN DO

"He is greatest whose strength carries up the most hearts by the attraction of his own."

—Henry Ward Beecher

The Moral Duty of Leaders

Leaders determine how we lead our lives and run our societies. Leaders have a great impact on how the world runs—whether that world is your family, your office, or your country. Leadership is responsible for changing the world.

The change can be good or bad. It's up to the leader to decide.

Treat Yourself

I spent decades trying to be what I thought my parents wanted me to be, and to study what I thought I was supposed to study, and to take the job I thought I was supposed to take.

I did all of this believing that I would somehow be taken care of and thrive if only I did what I was supposed to do.

Various people worried about me, and a few expressed concern, but no one knew how to help me thrive.

I found myself in yet another cubicle of yet another company and with more than just a little curiosity if this job would finally be right for me. I had a wife, two kids, a cat, a dog, and some of them looked to me for care and guidance, but I was convinced I could provide neither. I didn't even think I deserved to be happy.

Then I had my epiphany, and I began to care for my shadow-self. I have learned that if I try to nurture my shadow-self, I can offer care and guidance to others, as well.

So I've often wondered why those in a position of leadership so rarely offer care and guidance to those in their employ.

Treat Your Employees

It turns out that most so-called leaders are too busy struggling with their own problems to worry a whole heck of a lot about others. They become a butthead boss instead, using their position of power to get things done without concern for their employees' well-being.

They convene team meetings and demand status reports to suppress any and all resistance.

But, by practicing the most important things demanded of a leader, you will have access to the most effective form of leadership. You will escape the butthead, and demonstrate true leadership skills.

Lead Yourself

I believe there are five things that leaders must do well above all other things:

1. Care for yourself, so that you might lead by example.
2. Discover why the organization exists, and explain that to your team.
3. Develop other leaders, so that the strength of the organization may grow.
4. Set the emotional tone for your team.
5. Care for your team members as you care for yourself.

Care For Yourself

Caring for yourself, and especially your shadow-self, with compassion, allows you to continually reinforce the attributes and values that will present you to others as a leader worth following.

Discover What the Organization's Inner Child Needs to Thrive

Your organization exists for some purpose. But if bureaucracy has come to dominate the culture, or an obsession with performance is of primary concern, the quality of the product or service that your organization needs to sustain itself may be forgotten.

The purpose is to the organization what your inner child's desire is to you, and that purpose must be cared for and nurtured. All the members of the organization need to find at least part of their inspiration for doing good work in sustaining that purpose.

Develop Other Leaders

Developing the team's talent is how you improve your ability to care for and nurture the organization's purpose. And the highest form of that development is to recognize and support your team members' ability to develop their own leadership skills.

Your team's creativity grows as each member takes initiative to problem solve. It is the merging of each team member's talent and drive that sustains the organization's purpose.

Set the Emotional Tone for the Team

As a team leader, you have a unique vantage point on the scope of problems facing the team, the larger challenges of the organization, and the variety of skills each member brings to the table. It is incumbent upon you as a leader to find the emotional tone for your team that allows the best ideas to exist long enough that they may be used to solve your problems.

This requires a nearly constant consideration of how the team interactions and group dynamics affect individual performances. A lighter, more compassionate tone may be needed, but a different problem may require humor or deadpan seriousness.

Care for Your Team Members as You Care for Yourself

As I discussed in chapter 12, showing a sincere concern for others strengthens your relationship with them, and can inspire them to care for themselves, care for their team, and to be creative when solving problems.

This becomes a greater challenge for large teams, especially if you have risen in the ranks of the organization. But establishing development programs and benefits that allow team members to deal and cope with family or personal problems sends a clear message that you care.

Richard Teerlink (Harley Davidson CEO)

In the 1980s, Harley Davidson, a manufacturer of heavy motorcycles (hogs) so well known I can't believe I'm explaining them, was struggling to survive. Their market share had plummeted. To stay in business, they updated their manufacturing processes and inventory systems and established themselves as a viable entity once again. Their CFO during that time, Richard Teerlink, was named CEO in 1989 when it once again became a publicly traded company.

But Mr. Teerlink continued to search for ways to strengthen his company. Harley Davidson has now regained the majority of market share in their class of motorcycles. How did they do it?

Under Teerlink's leadership, they invested heavily in creating a learning environment to develop the skills of their workforce. They were convinced that the best way to differentiate themselves in the market, and to find competitive advantages, was to rely upon the talents of their entire organization ("Transformation at Harley-Davidson—University of Washington." 2006. 3 Dec. 2015)†.

Although there would be only one CEO for that time of recovery, they needed the leadership of as many people as possible, and created an environment where those leadership skills could develop.

The case study I cite did not emphasize the role of leadership training, so I am stretching a bit in using this example. However, I firmly believe that focusing on the core value that Harley Davidson provided to their customers was the organization's purpose. And the investment made by the company to create a learning environment empowered the employees to take part in the transformation.

We should all be so lucky to work at an organization that demonstrates this type of leadership and allows this degree of freedom.

15

IMPROVE LEADERSHIP AT YOUR ORGANIZATION IN A MEANINGFUL WAY

"Good leaders organize and align people around what the team needs to do. Great leaders motivate and inspire people with why they're doing it. That's purpose. And that's the key to achieving something truly transformational."

—Marillyn Hewson

But How Can I Do This Where I Work?

It may seem daunting to dare to change anything at your workplace. It may seem even more daunting to change yourself. Let's deal with the second one first.

We change all the time. I mentioned in chapter 7 that we become the average of the five people with whom we spend the most time. Change your posse, change yourself.

So get over the fact that you're changing: it's happening right now by reading this book.

Go ahead and think about how you want to change. Set your sails and tack into the wind.

If you work at a large business, the culture there is certainly well established, and there are well documented ways to make suggestions, and probably just as many undocumented ways to get things done.

Businesses are always solving problems, and if you can connect your own development, especially the development of your shadow-self, with the problems faced by the business, you will be able to exert influence and demonstrate leadership by sharing your ideas.

Small businesses may not have a well-established culture, but they often have a charismatic leader who is the de facto culture, not unlike what you might see in a mob drama like The Sopranos†. Regardless, there are still problems to solve, and connecting your leadership development with the business's problem will be a big step towards a sustainable solution.

I'm Tired of the Bullshit, I Just Want to do My Job

It is an on-going temptation to fall into a routine that doesn't challenge you to think very hard. In fact, the part of your brain that craves efficiency will demand that you do exactly that: figure out the easiest way to make your boss happy, do that, then repeat it over and over again.

I spent nearly two decades being clever at my job, finding ways to do the same thing faster and faster again, but not really developing any leadership skills of my own, or offering any game-changing ideas to my boss.

This style of non-leadership is increasingly risky in the modern workplace. Exhibiting that you have no leadership skills while not sharing any new ideas may turn the work you do into a commodity. You may be making it simple for your boss to find someone younger or cheaper to do your work.

The Solution

The key to job satisfaction is your relationship with your immediate boss. The person who assigns you work, tells you where to sit, and approves your time card. They have the power to make your work experience joyful or miserable.

Improving the leadership at your organization starts with improving your boss. So how does that happen?

Your boss may check to make sure that you are doing things right. But if you can tell your boss what is the right thing to be doing, your value increases.

Especially if you identify the right thing to do in order to make your boss's job easier, you have just endeared yourself to your boss, and so made your leadership better, your job more secure, and yourself more in control of your life.

Prescription

1. Make sure you are doing things right: filling out your time sheets, following procedures, and otherwise being a good employee. If you struggle to do the basics, your boss will be forced to use a less-than-transformational style of leadership on your ass.
2. Always, always, always take a moment to think about the customers when working on any assignment.
3. Find a way to discuss with your boss the right thing to do for the sake of your customers and the business.

4. Celebrate strong leadership. Find people that found the right thing to do and ask their advice.

What if You're a Big-Shot Kind of Boss?

The ability to listen to your team is critical. As a leader, you must set aside your ego (you're already the boss, so just chill) and your to-do list (you're going to delegate, anyway, so chill some more) and appreciate that at least one of your teammates is willing to share a problem with you.

It's all too easy for any of us to set problems aside, but if you're on a boat and there's a leak in the hull, the sooner you deal with that leak the better off everyone will be. No one wants to bear bad news to the boss, but it's critical you hear it directly from your team members. Make it as easy on them as possible, and thank them for the feedback.

Remind yourself that leadership is ultimately about service. If you can help your team solve their problems, you're doing your job. If you help them solve their problems in a way that matches your vision for success, and supports the purpose of your organization, you will help your team thrive.

Finally, if you are caring for yourself, discovering your purpose, setting the emotional tone, and developing other leaders, you are helping your organization thrive, regardless of the challenges and problems it may face.

16

BECOME THE LEADER YOU WERE MEANT TO BE

"The leader must know, must know that he knows, and must be able to make it abundantly clear to those around him that he knows."

—Clarence Randall

All Leaders Learned How to Lead

All the great (and also the terrible) leaders the world has ever known were made. They learned how to lead. They may have been born with certain attributes that helped them along the way, but they learned how to lead in their circumstances.

They just didn't know that they were learning "leadership."

You have the advantage, now, of using your natural inclination, figuring out what you do and don't know, and working towards developing the skills you need to succeed.

You get to set your own pace—be it fast or slow—and determine the path you walk.

Life is Too Random and Crazy for Anybody to Figure All of This Out

Before my epiphany, I was convinced that leaders were born, not made. I felt that way about all the skills and talents I admired. I thought the funniest people were born that way. I thought the best baseball players were born the best, and it was just a matter of time before they were discovered.

I truly believed that if you were great, and that your success was meant to be†, that some celestial talent scout would eventually get around to seeing your act, and then would tell the world.

I thought that about the monsters of the world, too. I thought Hitler, Stalin, and even Dick Cheney were born evil, and it was just a matter of time before the world was placed at their doorstep in a Faustian bargain. But no, they learned how to lead. It was just a question of what was inside of them that affected the world.

Strive to Improve Your Leader Skills Each Day

Arguably the most-often mentioned leaders of America were Abraham Lincoln and Benjamin Franklin. Both successful in their trade, and both sharing their talents with the nation and the world because of their ability to lead.

Their struggle to improve their talents is well-documented, often by their own hands. In their journals, letters, and (in Franklin's case) books, they describe the efforts, failures, and concerns for how they might keep improving. They also describe how they might make all the efforts worthwhile by helping others.

If it seems impossible to be the perfect leader to everybody, here is how to make it possible:

1. **GOAL**: Decide the type of leader you ultimately wish to be. Review the list of styles from
   earlier in this book, or refer to the Endnotes for
   references on other presentations. Or just
   Google them up, and you'll be offered a variety
   of interpretations.
2. **GAPS**: Inventory and audit your current skills
   to identify gaps. Take out a sheet of paper, and
   for each of the styles, write a few words about
   how effective you are. Highlight or circle those
   needing the most work. Give yourself a star at
   those you might already have figured out.
3. **ASSESS**: Match the gaps to your goal, watch-
   ing for quick wins (in order to build the habits
   needed). Decide which leadership styles might
   be useful.
4. **PLAN**: Create a plan covering the scope of your
   ultimate goal (use Evernote, pen and paper, or
   the SELF journal). The key requirement for this
   plan is that you can find it later on. Return to it
   that day, the next day, and so on. Life has a way
   of distracting us, and we need constant re-
   minders. What I like about the SELF journal is
   it's designed to be used, at a minimum, each
   morning and again in the evening. It will also be
   useful throughout the day. For your plan to succeed, you must return it back to the fore of your
   consciousness frequently. To use a cliché that
   was often said by a former boss of mine, "plan
   to work, and then work the plan."
5. **COMMIT**: Sign a contract with yourself to accomplish the plan and achieve your goal. This is
   also a design of the SELF journal, but I'd seen
   variations of this before. It sets a tone with

yourself, but the ritual of commitment is equally important. Ideally, share the commitment with someone else you trust to help align your priorities.

The benefits begin immediately, but the change may be small at first. Only through consistent effort will your brain adapt to these thought patterns, and improve your ability to care for yourself, care for others, and provide leadership when needed.

When the opportunity presents itself, you will be ready.

17

NEXT STEPS

"You got to be very careful if you don't know where you're going, because you might not get there."

—Yogi Berra

My Final Hope For You

If you're still worried about developing your leadership skills, remind yourself often that if you listen to your own heart and use self-compassion in solving your own problems, you are already far better off than most leaders. If you listen to other people's problems and offer help with sincere compassion, you are now better than 80% of the leaders† in the world.

Whether or not this leads to financial success, political power, or critical acclaim depends on a great many other factors beyond the scope of this book, and likely beyond your control.

But, I promise you will find solace and peace for yourself knowing that you have served others as you would serve yourself. And in so doing, you have made the world a better place.

Further Reading

The following books were particularly powerful to me:

- *Mindset: The New Psychology of Success*
- *The Talent Code: Greatness Isn't Born. It's Grown. Here's How*
- *The Tools: 5 Tools to Help You Find Courage, Creativity, and Willpower—and Inspire You to Live Life in Forward Motion*
- *Sapiens: A Brief History of Humankind*
- *Give and Take: Why Helping Others Drives Our Success*
- *The No Asshole Rule: Building a Civilized Workplace and Surviving One That Isn't*

Other References

One of the writers that led me to change (in a self-directed way) was Phillip J. Eby's articles†.

I have also been a Toastmasters† member for ten years, and I can attest to the ability public speaking has in developing your courage to confront challenges. You might also try a Dale Carnegie† course.

Heck, a good dog obedience trainer can probably do us all some good! When I took my dog, Blue, to class, I learned more about myself than I did about leading a dog.

18

A PARTING GIFT IN THANKS

I hope you enjoyed reading this book as much as I enjoyed writing it. More than that, I hope it helps you in some way with your life. My greatest desire is to make the world better with the stories I tell. Every little bit helps.

Free Gift

In appreciation of your taking the time to read this book, please visit my website at http://www.mickeyhadick.com/free-book where you will find a link for a free copy of one of my books.

That free book is the first self-help book I wrote, and it is more philosophical in nature. But I meant every word, and I hoped then as I do now to make the world a better place one book at a time.

I remain,
Mickey Hadick

19

ABOUT THE AUTHOR

Mickey Hadick lives near Lansing, Michigan where he has worked on short stories, novels, screenplays, and books for the past couple of decades.

He was born in Cleveland but left to learn Computer Engineering at the University of Michigan. He made his way back to Cleveland where he earned a Master of Computer and Information Science degree from Cleveland State, but ended up back in Michigan by way of Pennsylvania. Now he solves computer problems for an insurance company to earn a living, and lives with his wife, two children, and a cat or two.

If you enjoyed this book and would like to get in on deals for future books, join him at www.mickeyhadick.com.

20

ACKNOWLEDGMENTS

Josh Raab edited this book and really surprised me in how he challenged me to make it better. I was lucky to find him. This book is much improved under his guidance.

The cover design by Michael Reibsome is yet another example of some fine work by a skilled artist. I'd tell you how to contact him, but he's pretty busy. I'm better off for knowing him, and the book is better because of his skill.

Tom Matt, next door neighbor and business partner, is a constant source of inspiration. His work on a speech about leadership sparked an interest in me that led to this book.

Greg Hopkins was my second boss at Burroughs, and he stands out as one of my best bosses ever. He was smart and got things done, and he helped his team get things done, too. He also cared about us. I worked for him a second time at a different company, and he was still that good of a boss. Greg was also very understanding when it came to signing expense reports, and I am indebted to him for that.

MICKEY HADICK

I mentioned a few close people in my life that influenced me. I will do my best to thank them personally and to be worthy of their kindness.

21

REFERENCES

These are the links to the Internet from the text, gathered here for the print edition. The content of websites beyond the author's control are not his responsibility, nor that of the publisher. These references were accurate to the best of the author's ability at the time of writing this book.

Chapter 2
The journal I prefer for tracking activities can be found at Best Self: http://www.bestself.co/

The journal I prefer for expressing emotional thoughts is a Moleskine. The paper loves ink.

http://www.integrativepractitioner.com/index.php?option=com_content&view=article&id=1080

The Talent Code: Greatness Isn't Born. It's Grown. Here's How., by Daniel Coyle
April 28, 2009
Bantam; 1st edition (April 28, 2009)

https://en.wikipedia.org/wiki/Malcolm_Knowles

Maximize Your Quality Of Life, The 200% Solution, by Thomas Matt
Boomers Rock Media, LLC (October 15, 2012)
http://www.boomersrock.us/

The Progress Principle: Using Small Wins to Ignite Joy, Engagement, and Creativity by Teresa Amabile & Steven Kramer
Harvard Business Review Press; 1 edition (July 19, 2011)

Mindset: The New Psychology of Success, by Carol Dweck Ballantine Books; Reprint edition (December 26, 2007)

Chapter 3

Meditations: A New Translation by Marcus Aurelius
Modern Library (1900)

Peace Is Every Step: The Path of Mindfulness in Everyday Life, by Thich Nhat Hanh
Bantam (March 1, 1992)

Chapter 4

Getting Things Done: The Art of Stress-Free Productivity, by David Allen
Viking; 1st edition (January 8, 2001)

BOSS LESSONS

Master Your Workday Now!: Proven Strategies to Control Chaos, Create Outcomes, & Connect Your Work to Who You Really Are, by Michael Linenberger
New Academy Publishers; 1st edition (March 7, 2010)

Chapter 5
http://jamesclear.com/new-habit

http://www.bakadesuyo.com/2015/10/ritual/

The Winner's Brain: 8 Strategies Great Minds Use to Achieve Success, by Dr. Jeff Brown & Mark Fenske with Liz Neporent
Da Capo Lifelong Books; First Da Capo Press Edition (March 30, 2010)

Chapter 6
Memoirs Found in a Bathtub, by Stanislaw Lem
Andre Deutsch Ltd (August 13, 1992)

http://thoughtmedicine.com/2010/05/7-simple-ways-to-raise-your-happiness-set-point/

Chapter 7
http://www.businessinsider.com/jim-rohn-youre-the-average-of-the-five-people-you-spend-the-most-time-with-2012-7

Leadership: The Power of Emotional Intellegence, by Daniel Goleman
More Than Sound (2011)

Chapter 9

http://www.dalecarnegie.com/

https://www.toastmasters.org/

The Obstacle Is the Way: The Timeless Art of Turning Trials into Triumph, by Ryan Holiday
Portfolio (May 1, 2014)

Maximize Your Quality Of Life, The 200% Solution, by Thomas Matt
Boomers Rock Media, LLC (October 15, 2012)
http://www.boomersrock.us/

Think and Grow Rich, by Napoleon Hill
Alba & Tromm (September 17, 2010)

The Science of Hitting Paperback, by Ted Williams & John Underwood
Illustrated by Robert Cupp
Simon & Schuster; Revised edition (April 29, 1986)

The Tools: 5 Tools to Help You Find Courage, Creativity, and Willpower--and Inspire You to Live Life in Forward Motion, by Phil Stutz & Barry Michels
Spiegel & Grau (May 29, 2012)

BOSS LESSONS

Chapter 10

http://www.mickeyhadick.com/storytelling/dimaggio/

https://www.psychologytoday.com/blog/evil-deeds/201204/essential-secrets-psychotherapy-what-is-the-shadow

Chapter 11

http://gretchenrubin.com/about/

Chapter 13

Give and Take: Why Helping Others Drives Our Success, by Adam M. Grant
Penguin Books (April 9, 2013)

http://faculty.bschool.washington.edu/skotha/website/cases%20pdf/hd.pdf

Chapter 17

Mindset: The New Psychology of Success, by Carol Dweck
Ballantine Books; Reprint edition (December 26, 2007)

The Talent Code: Greatness Isn't Born. It's Grown. Here's How., by Daniel Coyle
Bantam; 1st edition (April 28, 2009)

The Tools: 5 Tools to Help You Find Courage, Creativity, and Willpower--and Inspire You to Live Life in Forward Motion, by Phil Stutz & Barry Michels

Spiegel & Grau (May 29, 2012)

Sapiens: A Brief History of Humankind, by Yuval
Noah Harari
Harper; 1st edition (February 10, 2015)

Give and Take: Why Helping Others Drives Our Success, by Adam M. Grant
Penguin Books (April 9, 2013)

The No Asshole Rule: Building a Civilized Workplace
and Surviving One That Isn't, by Robert I. Sutton
Business Plus; 1st edition (February 22, 2007)

http://dirtsimple.org/
https://www.toastmasters.org/
http://www.dalecarnegie.com/

My First Boss Stan

Around the office, we nicknamed him Stan the Man Unusual. It was a pun on Stan Musial, and was in tribute to his tell-it-like-it-is approach that contrasted sharply with our corporate etiquette. He was a nice guy to know.

The Talking Dog Joke

A man takes his dog, to a talent scout looking for work. "What can he do?" the talent scout asks. "He talks," says the man. "Alright, let's hear him say something," the talent scout says.

"What's on top of a house?" the man asks. "Roof," the dog says.

"What's on the side of a tree?" the man asks. "Bark," the dog says.

"And who's the greatest baseball player of all time?" "Ruth," the dog says.

"Alright, get out," the talent scout says. "You've had your fun now beat it."

The man and his dog are shown the door and look at each other on the sidewalk. "Well?" the dog asks. "Do you think I should have said Dimaggio?"

The Source of My Data

These are my estimates based on no data whatsoever. I'm just trying to get you to care for yourself, and hopefully care for others in order to make the world a better place to live, work, and die.

MICKEY HADICK

NOTES

MICKEY HADICK

NOTES

BOSS LESSONS

NOTES